T0301882

Cambridge Elements ≡

Elements in Development Economics
Series Editor-in-Chief
Kunal Sen
UNU-WIDER and University of Manchester

ESCAPING POVERTY TRAPS
AND UNLOCKING PROSPERITY
IN THE FACE OF CLIMATE RISK

Lessons from Index-Based Livestock Insurance

Nathaniel D. Jensen
University of Edinburgh

Francesco P. Fava
University of Milan

Andrew G. Mude
African Development Bank

Christopher B. Barrett
Cornell University

Brenda Wandera-Gache
African Management Institute

Anton Vrieling
University of Twente

Masresha Taye
Institute of Development Studies

Kazushi Takahashi
National Graduate Institute for Policy Studies

Felix Lung
World Bank

Munenobu Ikegami
Hosei University

Polly Ericksen
University of Vermont

Philemon Chelanga
Agency for Inclusive Innovations Development

Sommarat Chantarat
Puey Ungphakorn Institute for Economic Research, Bank of Thailand

Michael Carter
University of California – Davis

Hassan Bashir
Agency for Inclusive Innovations Development

Rupsha Banerjee
International Livestock Research Institute

Shaftesbury Road, Cambridge CB2 8EA, United Kingdom

One Liberty Plaza, 20th Floor, New York, NY 10006, USA

477 Williamstown Road, Port Melbourne, VIC 3207, Australia

314–321, 3rd Floor, Plot 3, Splendor Forum, Jasola District Centre, New Delhi – 110025, India

103 Penang Road, #05–06/07, Visioncrest Commercial, Singapore 238467

Cambridge University Press is part of Cambridge University Press & Assessment, a department of the University of Cambridge.

We share the University's mission to contribute to society through the pursuit of education, learning and research at the highest international levels of excellence.

www.cambridge.org
Information on this title: www.cambridge.org/9781009558242

DOI: 10.1017/9781009558280

© UNU-WIDER 2024

This publication is in copyright. Subject to statutory exception and to the provisions of relevant collective licensing agreements, with the exception of the Creative Commons version the link for which is provided below, no reproduction of any part may take place without the written permission of Cambridge University Press & Assessment.

An online version of this work is published at doi.org/10.1017/9781009558280 under a Creative Commons Open Access license CC-BY-NC-SA 3.0 IGO which permits re-use, distribution and reproduction in any medium for non-commercial purposes providing appropriate credit to the original work is given, any changes made are indicated, and the new work is published under the same licence terms. When the licensor is an intergovernmental organisation, disputes will be resolved by mediation and arbitration where possible. To view a copy of this license, visit https://creativecommons.org/licenses/by-nc-sa/3.0/igo

When citing this work, please include a reference to the DOI 10.1017/9781009558280

First published 2024

A catalogue record for this publication is available from the British Library.

ISBN 978-1-009-55824-2 Hardback
ISBN 978-1-009-55825-9 Paperback
ISSN 2755-1601 (online)
ISSN 2755-1598 (print)

Cambridge University Press & Assessment has no responsibility for the persistence or accuracy of URLs for external or third-party internet websites referred to in this publication and does not guarantee that any content on such websites is, or will remain, accurate or appropriate.

Escaping Poverty Traps and Unlocking Prosperity in the Face of Climate Risk

Lessons from Index-Based Livestock Insurance

Elements in Development Economics

DOI: 10.1017/9781009558280
First published online: June 2024

Nathaniel D. Jensen, Francesco P. Fava, Andrew G. Mude, and Christopher B. Barrett *et al.*

Author for correspondence: Nathaniel D. Jensen, njensen@ed.ac.uk

Abstract: This Element outlines the origins and evolution of an international award-winning development intervention, index-based livestock insurance (IBLI), which scaled from a small pilot project in Kenya to a design that underpins drought risk management products and policies across Africa. General insights are provided on (1) the economics of poverty, risk management, and drylands development; (2) the evolving use of modern remote sensing and data science tools in development; (3) the science of scaling; and (4) the value and challenges of integrating research with operational implementation to tackle development and humanitarian challenges in some of the world's poorest regions. This title is also available as Open Access on Cambridge Core.

Keywords: drought, index insurance, pastoralism, Africa, research for development

ISBNs: 9781009558242 (HB), 9781009558259 (PB), 9781009558280 (OC)
ISSNs: 2755-1601 (online), 2755-1598 (print)

Contents

1 Index-Based Livestock Insurance to Address Risk-Based Poverty Traps

Revisiting the Challenge of Persistent Poverty

When people's living standards fall below a minimum absolute or relative threshold that societies deem necessary to safeguard the dignity of human persons, they are typically labeled as "poor." Most cultures have sought to explain and reduce poverty, investing in the intrinsically normative topic with considerable moral authority (Iliffe 1987; Lipton & Ravallion 1995). Generations of scholars have sought to explain patterns of poverty and to identify interventions that might help reduce its tragic hold on humankind (Ravallion 2016).

A key empirical regularity throughout modern history is that poverty status varies more between places than within them, generating a large social science literature that documents and tries to explain spatially concentrated poverty (Lipton & Ravallion 1995; Jalan & Ravallion 2002; Bloom *et al.* 2003; Ravallion 2016). Dating back at least to Adam Smith (1776), economists have typically seen poverty as the natural consequence of insufficient accumulation of productive capital, and/or insufficiently advanced technologies to generate a stream of income from that capital sufficient to sustain adequate consumption of essential goods and services. Most poverty analysis starts from that conceptualization, pointing to spatial patterns of low capital accumulation and anemic rates of adoption of modern technologies – both often arising due to market failures, especially in finance – to explain widespread, deep poverty. Others take a more radical view of poverty, which they see as the natural result of surplus extraction from the weak by the powerful (Watts 1983; Iliffe 1987).

The poorest places on Earth are defined not only by the prevalence and depth of the poverty residents experience but also by the persistence of that poverty (Barrett & Swallow 2006). Poverty analysis has advanced considerably as longitudinal data on the same households and individuals have become more widespread (Carter & Barrett 2006; Barrett *et al.* 2016). The evolving poverty dynamics literature consistently finds that an identifiable subpopulation disproportionally suffers sustained deprivation that others never experience.

Normative concerns about persistent poverty have long motivated research on "poverty traps," which are defined as an absorbing state of persistent poverty. A large body of literature on poverty traps has focused on why low levels of capital accumulation and failure to adopt advanced technologies might be self-reinforcing equilibria (Azariadis & Stachurski 2005; Barrett & Swallow 2006; Bowles *et al.* 2006; Kraay & McKenzie 2014; Barrett *et al.* 2016). Poverty traps have typically been modeled as low-level equilibria that arise from coordination (including market) failures with a focus on deterministic systems (Dasgupta 1997; Mookherjee & Ray 2002; Azariadis & Stachurski 2005; Ghatak 2015). Many poverty trap narratives and models have a Sisyphean character to them, in which people placed in impossible situations are doomed because desirable outcomes are simply unattainable. Rags-to-riches stories excite the popular imagination in part because they offer hope of escape from poverty traps, even if one's odds of success are slim.

The more recent literature on poverty traps dispenses with old, deterministic assumptions and focuses instead on the central role that risk plays in persistent poverty (Barrett *et al.* 2019). A deep, and influential literature documents the poor's considerable exposure to risk and the limited market- or technology-based tools they have available to mitigate risk (Stiglitz 1974; Fafchamps 2003; Dercon 2004)

The newer framing of risk-based poverty traps follows from the observation that another defining feature of places with high rates of deep, persistent poverty is disproportionate exposure to uninsured, catastrophic risk, often from multiple sources such as weather, markets, disease, and conflict. For example, across a range of societies at different stages of development, uninsured health shocks are consistently the single greatest cause of descent into persistent poverty (Krishna 2010), consistent with the literature that highlights how infectious disease risk exposure can trap individuals, or even entire communities, in long-term poverty (Bonds *et al.* 2010; Ngonghala *et al.* 2014; Ngonghala *et al.* 2017). This newer literature elevates the value of effective risk management to a status comparable to that of capital accumulation and improved technology adoption as central to enabling sustained improvements in living conditions (Barrett *et al.* 2019). In this view, deep, persistent poverty is not solely the consequence of bad initial conditions but rather of the combination of poor circumstances and excessive exposure to adverse shocks.

Some poverty traps feature multiple equilibria wherein any individual[1] may either escape poverty or collapse to an absorbing state of persistent poverty, depending only on their initial wealth and the sequence of shocks that they experience. Such a system generates what Ikegami *et al.* (2019) call "unnecessary deprivation," which occurs when individuals who have the capacity and means to be nonpoor are rendered poor by risk and shocks. Providing such individuals with better risk management tools should in principle reduce unnecessary deprivation and create substantial social and economic gains. Even for individuals who can in principle eventually escape poverty, risks and

---

[1] Individual here can mean a single person, but also a single or even more complex family unit.

shocks lower their expected long-term well-being, slow their advance to improved living conditions, and generate costly transitory poverty. Better risk management tools can offer substantial social and economic gains for such people as well.

Persistent Poverty in East Africa's Arid and Semiarid Lands

Index-based livestock insurance (IBLI) was conceived, launched, studied, and adapted within the context of the longstanding struggle to understand and reduce persistent poverty in a specific place: the arid and semiarid lands (ASALs) of East Africa.[2] In many ways, this is an archetypal region, characterized by widespread, deep, persistent poverty among populations routinely buffeted by a range of potentially catastrophic shocks. ASALs are the largest globally by area, covering roughly one-third of the Earth's land surface, and host over one billion people, who commonly are pastoralists whose livelihoods predominantly rely on livestock production, often involving extensive grazing on communal lands, whereby seasonal movement in search of forage and water is important (de Leeuw *et al.* 2019). In relatively more humid ASAL areas, agropastoralists combine livestock with rainfed crop production (Nidumolu *et al.* 2022).

Livestock are pastoralists' main store of wealth; a productive asset that generates a plurality of community income and consumption goods, offers social status, and underpins many cultural rituals. Livestock are pastoralists' main nonhuman productive asset and the production technologies involved in extensive grazing are few. In many ways, this makes pastoralist populations ideal for the study of stochastic poverty dynamics and the search to explain and unlock risk-based poverty traps.

The decade-long, multidisciplinary Pastoral Risk Management (PARIMA) project set out to study such populations in the ASALs of northern Kenya and neighboring southern Ethiopia.[3] The project identified the strong influence of drought risk on more salient food security and human health risks, which households perceive and attempt to manage (Smith *et al.* 2000; Barrett *et al.* 2001; Little *et al.* 2001; McPeak & Barrett 2001; Doss *et al.* 2008). A series of papers found that drought shocks led to considerable, avoidable human suffering and that existing policy responses – mainly relief food shipped from distant countries – were slow to arrive and ineffective in mitigating the most serious

---

[2] IBLI provides insurance against unusually low remote sensing (satellite) measures of forage availability that are strongly correlated with livestock productivity and mortality. Section 3 explains index insurance in greater depth. Sections 4 and beyond explain the particulars of IBLI in detail.

[3] McPeak *et al.* (2011) summarize many findings of that research project.

human consequences that emerged from droughts (Mude *et al.* 2009; Nikulkov *et al.* 2016).

Among the important findings from the PARIMA project, multiple data sets clearly established the existence of poverty traps in these communities (McPeak & Barrett 2001; Lybbert *et al.* 2004; Barrett *et al.* 2006; Santos & Barrett 2011). Multiple data sets consistently identified a threshold of 6–12 Tropical Livestock Units (TLUs),[4] above which pastoralists could viably maintain large herds through transhumant or rotational grazing, and below which herd size collapsed to a low-level equilibrium of roughly one cow as it became infeasible to sustain the mobility required to sustain a larger herd (Lybbert *et al.* 2004; Barrett *et al.* 2006; Santos & Barrett 2011; Barrett & Santos 2014; Toth 2015). Moreover, the work established that uninsured catastrophic drought risk exposure is the primary cause of those poverty traps (Santos & Barrett 2019) and increases in the frequency of catastrophic drought due to climate change threaten to close off the high-level equilibrium options that remain, leading to system collapse (Barrett & Santos 2014).

The drought risk-based poverty traps framing of the persistent poverty suffered by so many of the region's pastoralists also helped explain why standard interventions often failed in the long-term. Post-drought restocking, for example, rarely restored herd sizes to the point where households regained the ability to migrate seasonally, and the frequency of drought meant that herds could rarely grow to a viable size before the next drought struck (Toth 2015; Santos & Barrett 2019). Meanwhile, emergency food aid and other transfers commonly failed to equip poor households to build assets, nor did they prevent collapse into destitution for formerly nonpoor pastoralists who had lost much of their herd due to a catastrophic drought, swelling the involuntarily sedentarized subpopulations in ASAL towns that increasingly overwhelmed underfunded social protection programs (Ikegami *et al.* 2019). New tools were clearly needed to help pastoralists manage catastrophic drought risk. IBLI was initially developed as a microinsurance scheme for pastoralists in an ASAL system characterized by multiple equilibrium poverty traps. However, its effectiveness as a drought risk management tool drew broader interest as a scalable risk management instrument applicable to individuals and households at the micro level, among governments at the macro scale, as well as a range of meso-scale organizations in between.

---

[4] TLUs allow aggregation across livestock species based on body mass and nutrient intake requirements. For East Africa, ILRI deems one adult cow weighing 250 kg equivalent to 1.0 TLU, a camel equivalent to 1.4 TLUs, and sheep and goats each equivalent to 0.1 TLU.

Conventional forms of social assistance, whether emergency food aid or cash transfers, are reactive as they respond only to the needs of those who have already collapsed into unnecessary deprivation. They do not address the underlying structural causes that generate that collapse, nor necessarily help individuals maintain resilience to withstand and recover from shocks, or even advance economically in their wake.

We set out to identify alternative interventions that might work better than those conventional mechanisms. Index-based risk transfer products were seen as a potential instrument for unlocking poverty traps, both by preventing descents into poverty and by inducing productivity-increasing investment and lending to facilitate such investment (Chantarat *et al.* 2007; Barnett *et al.* 2008; Chantarat *et al.* 2011; Chantarat *et al.* 2013; Chantarat *et al.* 2017). We designed an IBLI product with the intention to reduce negative impacts from drought risk and thereby to facilitate escapes from the poverty traps among the region's residents. Similar objectives motivated parallel efforts elsewhere, as a range of agricultural index insurance products were designed in various settings to try to reduce risks associated with extreme weather events (as explained in greater detail in Section 3). A similarly named IBLI product emerged at roughly the same time in Mongolia, albeit with a different design and aimed at extreme weather events rather than droughts (Mahul & Skees 2007; Bertram-Huemmer & Kraehnert 2018). For a range of reasons explained in the coming sections, the East African IBLI product has generated greater – or at least better documented – impacts and diffused more broadly than most other agricultural index insurance products, which have largely remained pilots or small-scale projects (Carter *et al.* 2017).

Although social gains from financial risk management tools that disrupt poverty traps can be high (see Section 3), financial innovation needs to satisfy three key requirements. First, it must be high quality, so it reliably delivers payments when needed. Second, it must deliver assistance speedily during or near the onset of a shock to prevent individuals from losing or depleting their assets (e.g., through distress sales or abandonment with migration). Third, it must be trusted such that individuals will shift their behavior in advance of indemnity payments.

These triple requirements of quality, speed, and trust informed our approach to developing IBLI. We hypothesized that these goals could be more easily attained with a pre-financed commercial contract than through a politically mediated transfer process that would always be subject to the vagaries of public sector budgets and politicians' short-run interests. These challenges of quality, speed, and trust required both excellent product design, aided by the emergence of new remote sensing techniques and technologies (see Section 5), as well as strong partnerships between researchers and operational agencies, both commercial and public, to continuously adapt the product and its outreach (see Sections 4, 6, and 8).

As an experiment, IBLI had two distinctive characteristics. Firstly, launching IBLI required collaboration with commercial reinsurers, underwriters, retail agents, and a wide range of social and environmental scientists, as well as international donors, national and local governments, communities, and non-profit partners. The resulting partnerships brought together organizations and individuals with markedly different motivations to develop, adapt, and diffuse IBLI. This posed major management challenges but also broadened insights and ultimately buy-in to IBLI as the original design proved successful (Banerjee *et al.* 2019; Johnson *et al.* 2019).

Secondly, IBLI needed rigorous impact evaluation. Did it really obviate the adverse, especially the catastrophic, impacts of drought? Did IBLI induce behavioral responses by pastoralist households and communities emboldened to risk scarce investible resources into economic advancement? Did it reduce descents into poverty, facilitate escapes from poverty traps, and generally boost welfare? And was it cost-effective in doing so, especially as compared to popular alternative investments, such as cash transfer programs? What programmatic and design lessons could be learned to inform the scaling of risk management tools more broadly, beyond just the original IBLI product and the specific place where it originated?

These are among the many questions that this Element will address. Before doing that, it is essential to understand the social and environmental setting of IBLI's place-specific origins in tackling the challenge of risk-based poverty traps.

2 East African Pastoralism: Change and Variability

The 300 million or so Africans who inhabit ASALs face serious challenges. The compounding effects of natural and environmental factors – such as unpredictable weather and spatially variable soil quality – policy and politics, and infrastructure make pastoralism in East Africa a risky endeavor. Droughts, the most common severe shock that hits ASALs, are often correlated with other shocks (e.g., conflict, disease, macroeconomic) and commonly cause catastrophic loss of wealth and income for many people within affected communities, frequently leading to humanitarian disasters. IBLI was designed to insure against drought, a "covariate shock" that affects large areas (distinct from "idiosyncratic shocks" that strike just one or a few families at a time), and specifically for pastoralists in an area straddling the Ethiopia-Kenya border in East Africa.

Climate is a key determinant of rangeland productivity, as vegetation growth follows rainfall amount, frequency, and duration (Coppock 1994; Coppock *et al.* 2017). Forage and water availability drive variability in ASAL livestock production. Pastoralism has evolved over centuries to manage the spatial and temporal variability of water and pasture.

A key defining feature of East Africa's ASALs is low and highly variable rainfall, with a bimodal seasonal pattern in most cases. These areas typically receive as little as 200 to 300 mm of rainfall annually, and rarely more than 600 mm (Williams & Funk 2011). Unpredictable rainfall patterns, combined with calcareous soils of low carbon and mineral content (Homewood 2008), result in low crop yield potential and render crop agriculture unreliable. Livelihoods therefore depend heavily on extensive grazing of cattle, camels, goats, and sheep. Livestock enable sporadic crop cultivation – mainly of maize – as the animals import essential soil nutrients and water by grazing elsewhere and then concentrating manure and urine within overnight enclosures that people can subsequently farm. During periods of good rains and availability of inputs, pastoralists often diversify into crop cultivation as a temporary relief and a means of supporting livestock, at least on stover (Catley *et al.* 2013). Even so, crop yields remain low and crop failures are commonplace.

Because they are central to pastoralist livelihoods, livestock is equally central to pastoralists' individual and community identities. Livestock ownership is not just a store of wealth but is equally a centerpiece of sociocultural activities and a leading source of social status. Livestock and their products are embedded in a variety of rituals and ceremonies, beginning with a person's birth, and continuing through their circumcision, marriage, childbirth, and passing.

Complex usufruct rules and agreements traditionally allowed pastoralists the flexibility they needed to ensure access to precious dry season reserves. However, this same flexibility also makes pastoralists vulnerable to land loss and exclusion from customary ranges (Homewood 2008). In recent decades, spatial expansion of towns and cultivated farmlands, as well as the gazetting of protected areas, have increased land fragmentation and increased exclusive uses for purposes other than grazing, reducing pastoralists' ability to access crucial grazing and water reserves (Galvin *et al.* 2002; Munyao & Barrett 2007). Heavy grazing from restricted mobility can also degrade rangelands (Galvin *et al.* 2002) and threaten their sustainability. In addition, woody shrubs are expanding across rangelands because of both management practices and increases in carbon and nitrogen emissions (Galvin *et al.* 2002). Proliferation of woody cover (or "bush encroachment") has been compounded by governments' (including Ethiopia's) misunderstanding of the role of fire in mesic savanna ecosystems, resulting in ill-advised, strict fire bans that enable woody species to expand, degrading rangeland productivity and biodiversity (Johansson *et al.* 2021). The introduction of the fast-growing, non-native woody species *Prosopis juliflora* in ASAL environmental rehabilitation programs has likewise caused considerable damage in many rangelands, generating conflict between conservationists and pastoralists and lawsuits for damages caused by the *Prosopis* (Maundu *et al.* 2009).

On top of increasingly restricted land and water access, droughts seem to have grown more frequent and severe in recent decades. Rainfall variability increases with aridity and climate change in this region (Overpeck & Udall 2020). The bimodal pattern in most of the Horn of Africa brings "short rains" from October to December and "long rains" from March to May. The "short" rains exhibit more interannual variability and are especially affected by El Niño Southern Oscillation (ENSO) events (Mutai & Ward 2000), with El Niño years bringing more precipitation and La Niña bringing less. Unfortunately, La Niña events are growing more frequent with global warming (Cai *et al.* 2015). Indian Ocean temperature anomalies can also influence precipitation in the absence of an ENSO event (Zhao & Cook 2021; Doi *et al.* 2022).

Analysis of decadal rainfall trends in East Africa showed significant declines in long rains precipitation and increased unpredictability in the region between 1960 and 2009 (Williams & Funk 2011). Liebmann *et al.* (2014) found that the short rainy season has become wetter while the long rains are drier, but the significant increase in the short rains is compromised by strong year-to-year fluctuations. Ayugi *et al.* (2022) projected more frequent, longer, and stronger intensity droughts in this ASAL region in the future. These patterns – and the associated potential for system collapse (Barrett & Santos 2014) – underpin the need for regular revisiting of IBLI product design and pricing (see Section 5).

In severe or prolonged droughts, livestock mortality rates increase sharply. Livestock population dynamics are determined by short-term losses during drought and longer-term trends in resource conditions, thus it can take several years for a herd to recover after a major drought and longer if several rainy seasons fail (as has been the case recently) and herd mobility is constrained. Significant droughts struck the region in 2011, 2014, 2016–2017, 2019, and 2021–2022, and the popular perception is droughts are becoming more severe in their impacts (Funk *et al.* 2015; Ayugi, Eresanya *et al.* 2022).

Pastoral communities have long been marginalized by colonial and postcolonial central governments. Pastoral systems are socioculturally alien to the foreign and highland populations that have long dominated Ethiopia, Kenya, and other countries in the region. Few colonists or postcolonial leaders wanted to live in the harsher ASAL regions. Therefore, the infrastructure and institutions created to serve leaders' (and their core constituencies') own needs were concentrated outside the ASALs. Governments have often supported, explicitly or implicitly, the privatization of communal pastoralists grazing areas, gazetting protected areas or mining concessions, and even enclosures of rangelands previously held in common property with overlapping access rights among groups. Meanwhile, the central state has been notably absent in offering police protection, which contributes to a widespread sense of lawlessness in these ASALs (Catley & Iyasu 2010; Wild *et al.* 2019; Lind *et al.* 2020).[5] Even when trying to help pastoralists, insufficient understanding of the rationale for and logic of pastoralism has often led to misguided development interventions, especially with respect to market development, rangeland rehabilitation, and early warning.

Perhaps the most tangible material manifestation of pastoralists' marginalization is their relative lack of infrastructure. They have fewer schools, fewer health facilities, limited electricity or telecommunications connectivity, insufficient water, and sanitation facilities, and fewer maintained or all-season roads (McPeak *et al.* 2011). Indeed, the last stretch of the pan-African highway – which stretches from Egypt to South Africa – to get hard surface paving (e.g., asphalt or concrete) was in northern Kenya. The lack of roads, electricity, and so on, makes manufacturing and services difficult and hampers private investments in the livestock sector, such as in slaughterhouses, canneries, dairy processing plants, and other value addition services.

As ASAL populations live far from the major cities, this marginalization has been easy to ignore. This is changing in Kenya and Ethiopia, albeit slowly. Moreover, change is not always driven by communities' best interests, as with improvements made in northern Kenya connected to (largely foreign-financed) hydrocarbons exploration and trade infrastructure (e.g., the Lamu Port, South Sudan, Ethiopia Transport) LAPSSET corridor through Isiolo and oil discovery in Turkana).

Beginning in the late 2000s, however, mobile telephone service began in parts of southern Ethiopia and northern Kenya. Inexpensive phones and services offered unprecedented connectivity to distant markets and financial services such as mobile banking and digital payments. Communication is now much easier, and households can send and receive money, reducing two major impediments faced by these populations in prior years (McPeak *et al.* 2011).

---

[5] As Wild *et al.* (2019) explain, pastoralists' underrepresentation in national and global health statistics is another form of marginalization, especially because those statistics are used to direct public funds.

East Africa's rangelands are also home to large and diverse wildlife populations, attracting tourists from around the globe. Until the past few decades, wildlife coexisted with domesticated livestock, as both populations moved across the rangelands as seasons changed. In Kenya, two-thirds of the wildlife population are found in communal lands, groups, and private ranches (Western *et al.* 2009) rather than in nationally protected areas. The importance of working with pastoral communities to maintain wildlife populations is generally recognized (Reid *et al.* 2016; Western *et al.* 2020). However, community-based or other forms of inclusive tourism enterprises may not benefit all community members. Competition over land and other resources remains a key challenge, especially when protected areas exclude pastoral livestock, and as other development schemes and urbanization take up land and fence off mobility corridors (Munyao & Barrett 2007). Although there is considerable evidence that wildlife and livestock can be managed together, implementation of that model is not widespread, and too often wildlife conservationists – including large-scale private ranches that support ecotourism, conservancies, or similar services – and pastoralists engage in conflict over land tenure. Beyond contestation over land rights, herd movement has often induced inter-clan and inter-ethnic conflict with sedentarized populations, environmental conservation agencies, or both (Bassi 2005).

The overlap between wildlife and livestock populations also produces disease interactions, although pastoralists have traditionally known when to move animals to avoid vector-borne diseases that increase with rains. Governments since the colonial era have been quick to impose quarantines on pastoral areas when infectious disease outbreaks occur, protecting the highland herds around the major cities at considerable cost to pastoralists and the traders who intermediate between the ASALs and the highlands (Barrett *et al.* 2003). Advocates of One Health approaches – which recognize that the health of people, animals, plants, and the environment are interdependent – argue for studying and managing healthy animals, people, and ecosystems in a more integrated fashion, especially emphasizing its benefits for pastoralists (Greter *et al.* 2014).

The compounding effect of natural risks – poor soils, variable rainfall, frequent droughts, livestock, and human disease – and manmade ones arising from weak property rights in land and water (McCarthy *et al.* 2000), weak infrastructure, and political marginalization confront pastoralists with considerable uninsured covariate risk from drought and disease among others. Governments and donors have historically mounted slow and insufficient responses to such disasters, mainly food aid shipments and limited post-drought restocking (Mude *et al.* 2009; Nikulkov *et al.* 2016; Santos & Barrett 2019).

The increasing frequency and severity of droughts, and the absence of adequate social protection response, have led to mass livestock mortality events that leave millions of pastoralists vulnerable to collapse into poverty traps (Lybbert *et al.* 2004; Barrett *et al.* 2006; Santos & Barrett 2019). IBLI was initially developed in this context, as a tool for pastoral populations to protect themselves from poverty traps that originate in drought risk. As we explain in subsequent sections, as IBLI spread to a wider range of countries, the changing context has necessitated adapting the product design (e.g., from predicted livestock mortality to forage scarcity) and delivery channels, as well as its scaling.

3 Index-Based Insurance for Pastoralist Regions

Index insurance offers a prospective solution to poor rural communities' exposure to the risk of extreme weather events (Barnett *et al.* 2008), inspiring a range of efforts to develop products well-suited to specific contexts (Carter *et al.* 2017; Jensen & Barrett 2017). This section explains the basic logic of index-based insurance in general and how this logic has been implemented for IBLI in East Africa's ASALs specifically to address the covariate drought shocks pastoralists face, and to leverage markets to cost-effectively transfer the systemic drought risk characterizing the region.

The potential of IBLI in these pastoralist regions extends far beyond simply exploiting a financial tool for solving a risk management failure. Conventional humanitarian aid and social protection programs, such as cash transfers and relief food distribution, commonly react to people falling into poverty. In targeting those that are already poor, such programs do not prevent people's collapse into poverty nor dismantle the structural forces that generate chronic poverty in the first place. This section also explores the additional economic logic for index insurance for individuals and as a complement to existing social protection programming in these drought-prone regions characterized by poverty traps.

Index Insurance and its Strengths and Weaknesses

Insurance products can provide an adaptive, market-based solution to help manage risks. In advanced market economies, households and businesses typically seek – and sometimes are legally obliged to hold – insurance against catastrophic losses to prime income-earning assets such as life, health, or property (including automobile and home).[6] Such insurance contracts are

---

[6] Globally, life insurance accounts for roughly 45% of all premiums, while health insurance and property and casualty account for roughly one-quarter each (Binder *et al.* 2021). The insurance industry is built around insuring assets, not annual income flows from assets. Hence the need for

traditionally designed as indemnity insurance, in other words as contracts that reimburse policyholders in the event of a verifiable loss they incur. In the context of livestock insurance, examples include several of the plans available in the United States through the United States Department of Agriculture's Risk Management Agency.

In some settings, conventional indemnity insurance designs may not be commercially feasible because of incentive problems associated with moral hazard and adverse selection[7] and high transaction costs to monitor policyholders' behavior and verify their loss claims. This is especially true in places like East Africa's ASALs, where most of the population lives in remote locations and where their limited wealth restricts the sums insured. As such, the fixed costs of information verification make it nearly impossible to profitably offer conventional contracts. Hazell (1992) offers several striking examples of conventional loss-adjusted contracts where the insurance provider cannot cost-effectively verify losses, with national insurance programs from the 1980s paying out two to five times the premiums collected, a financially unsustainable design.

Index insurance products can fill the gap left by this market failure for conventional insurance contracts.[8] Index insurance employs a cheap-to-measure "index" that correlates with individual losses, but that cannot be meaningfully influenced by any party to the contract. For example, a suitable index could be a river's water level to approximate a household's flood-related damages. Index insurance can thereby avoid moral hazard and adverse selection problems because loss verification is independent of the behavior and type of the insured. Index insurance can also significantly reduce transaction costs to generate risk profiles, set appropriate premium rates, and verify losses by using an index available at low cost in near-real time. In the case of IBLI, the index is based on remote sensing (satellite) measures of forage availability that are strongly correlated with livestock productivity and mortality (see Section 5). In the ASAL context, index insurance obviates the asymmetric information and costly loss verification problems that render conventional indemnity insurance infeasible, opening the door to offering commercial insurance to low-wealth households in remote locations.

Despite the benefits of index insurance, it has several weaknesses. First, the use of an index that is only correlated with, but not identical to, individual

---

government subsidization in order for crop, unemployment or other forms of term-specific income insurance to be viable.

[7] Adverse selection occurs when clients purchase insurance that is offered at premium rates that are set using estimates of the client's risk that are lower than they actually face. Moral hazard arises when having insurance induces behavioral change, in particular that the client engages in riskier behavior because they no longer bear the full cost of all potential adverse outcomes.

[8] See Carter *et al.* (2017) for a review.

losses, also opens the door to "basis risk," including both "false negatives" – a pastoralist who suffered a drought-related loss is not indemnified because the index failed to signal it – and "false positives" – a pastoralist who has not had losses is indemnified as if they had. False positives raise the premium cost of insurance (Elabed *et al.* 2013; Carter & Chiu 2018a). Jensen *et al.* (2016) evaluated the first IBLI index, which was used from 2010 until 2015, and found that it covered only 31 percent of households' herd mortality risk, with the remainder lost to index imperfections that relate to differences between household-specific and area-average rates of livestock mortality. The index was revised in 2015 to allow payouts to take place earlier, before drought impacts have been fully realized. While Jensen *et al.* (2019) found that the new index correlated well with covariate livestock mortality observations, it has not been evaluated comprehensively for basis risk since then (see Section 5).

Second, compared to conventional indemnity-based insurance, index insurance products are also relatively complex financial instruments from a policyholder perspective. Not only do they require an understanding of basic insurance mechanics, financial planning, and trust in the insurance provider, but add the complexity of understanding and accepting an index which, in the case of IBLI, is observed from space, and is subject to the mentioned basis risk. Low financial literacy among pastoralists in the ASALs may limit index insurance demand (Patt *et al.* 2009), although evidence suggests that an accurate understanding of IBLI contract terms has only a limited effect on demand (Takahashi *et al.* 2016; Jensen *et al.* 2018).

Finally, although index insurance sharply reduces underwriters' costs of claim verification, the sales and indemnity distribution costs of an active insurance distribution network nonetheless remain high in remote rural areas, driving up premium rates. Data from one IBLI underwriter in Kenya show that for every United States dollar (USD) collected in IBLI premium, it cost on average USD 1.26 in operations and USD 1.76 in payouts, that is, about USD 3 in total to administer the policy (Lung *et al.* 2021). As many of these are fixed costs, this underscores the importance of market development efforts to get to a commercially viable scale (Section 6).

Economic Logic for Micro-level Index Insurance in Pastoralist Areas

Index insurance can help resolve conventional insurance market failures, especially if care is taken with product design and quality control (Carter *et al.* 2017; Jensen & Barrett 2017). Products like IBLI that aim to ensure productive assets may be even more viable than index insurance products that aim to insure annual income realizations, consistent with the observation that most insurance policies globally insure assets, not income streams. This underlines the logic for index insurance; it can resolve an important financial market failure faced by poor households in rural areas.

Potentially the most important added value of index insurance in contexts like East Africa's ASALs comes from the role it can play in the presence of a risk-based poverty trap. In the rest of this section, we consider the economic case for even imperfect index insurance as a social protection tool to alter poverty dynamics in pastoral regions.

Uninsured catastrophic drought risk exposure is the core mechanism that drives pastoralists into poverty traps (Lybbert *et al.* 2004; Barrett *et al.* 2006; Santos & Barrett 2019). Against this backdrop, IBLI was introduced in the Marsabit district of northern Kenya in January 2010 and the Borana plateau of southern Ethiopia in August 2012. When a subset of the authors of this Element approached potential funders to support the design and piloting of IBLI, we hypothesized that IBLI would offer a higher benefit–cost ratio and would result in lower long-term social protection expenditures than the usual mix of food aid and regular cash transfers targeted at the already-poor. In simple terms, we argued that a USD 15 annual insurance subsidy for vulnerable households would prove cheaper than letting the vulnerable slip into chronic poverty where they would become eligible for a USD 15 per-month cash transfer.

That intuition has been developed more formally in a sequence of papers (Carter & Ikegami 2009; Ikegami *et al.* 2019; Janzen *et al.* 2021) that establish that index insurance can indeed reduce the total cost of social protection through two key mechanisms. The first is a "vulnerability reduction effect." Insurance can protect households' assets against catastrophic losses and maintain their economic viability at a relatively low cost, reducing the risk that they become chronically poor and require ongoing social protection expenditures. The second is an "investment incentive effect." Insurance enhances households' incentive to prudentially invest more in productive assets, making it less likely that they will require social protection assistance in the future.

Those studies find that small herd sizes – those below the 6–12 TLU threshold identified before – whether initially or following a shock, can trap chronic poverty households who would otherwise grow their herds and not be poor, generating an "unnecessarily deprived" subpopulation due to some combination of low initial livestock wealth, misfortune, or both. IBLI was designed to change these poverty dynamics. It provides a safety net to the nonpoor who suffer drought-related herd mortality shocks that might otherwise cast them into unnecessary deprivation in the longer term. At the same time, IBLI can induce more investment by initially poor households by reducing the risk that they lose that investment in the next drought. This generates a "paradox of social protection," reflecting the dynamic trade-offs that arise in a world of risk and poverty traps (Ikegami *et al.* 2019). The social protection paradox arises when concentrating exclusively on the most destitute and ignoring the vulnerable, near- or barely poor leads to worse outcomes eventually for the poorest. The reason is that one needs to invest in preventing shocks, like droughts, from casting people unnecessarily into destitution else the ultra-poor population grows and overwhelms limited humanitarian budgets and ultimately harms the poorest relative to what could have been achieved by balancing humanitarian assistance with effective risk management (Ikegami *et al.* 2019). Therefore, besides offering an important risk management instrument in settings characterized by poverty traps, IBLI can also provide a cost-effective means to address vulnerability and the structural forces that generate chronic poverty. Most of those gains come from the vulnerability reduction effect. If in addition, the insurance is subsidized using a loosely targeted program, long-term poverty falls further, primarily due to the investment incentive effect, which leads some previously poor households to escape poverty. These results based on empirical data and micro-level simulations have helped stimulate demand for IBLI also at the macro scale.

Economic Logic for Macro-level Index Insurance

IBLI was developed and rolled out as a micro-level insurance product, that is, one sold directly to individual pastoralists. But index insurance can also be used at the macro level where it is purchased by national or sub-national governments, or by nongovernmental development or humanitarian organizations (Fava *et al.* 2021; Lung *et al.* 2021). In settings characterized by poverty traps, the logic of the preceding section can make index insurance an attractive policy instrument for combatting catastrophic risk, ensuring social protection in the face of shocks like droughts, and inducing private investment.

Two subcategories of IBLI macro-level programs have been implemented to date. One is IBLI as a sovereign risk insurance program where governments purchase the policy and receive payouts which they commit to deploy based on a pre-agreed response plan to mitigate the impact of the insured risk. In 2021 African Risk Capacity (ARC) Ltd., a specialized agency of the African Union, added a pastoral component to the portfolio of products it offers African governments prioritizing coverage for pastoral regions, with a similar design as IBLI. The second is a "modified macro product," which is basically the micro-scale IBLI aggregated into bulk purchases of the policy by institutions on behalf of individual households who directly receive any indemnity payout if the index triggers. This approach was piloted by the Government of Kenya via the Kenya Livestock Insurance Program (KLIP) and by the World Food Programme (WFP) in the Satellite Index Insurance for Pastoralists in Ethiopia (SIIPE) program. Sections 4 and 5 provide further details on these programs.

Macro-level programs can help overcome the weaknesses of index insurance outlined earlier. First, the ARC-type macro product eliminates the idiosyncratic risk component of basis risk for the policy holder (e.g., a government) because individual household-specific risks cancel each other out. Modified macro products, by enrolling more households, can help support informal insurance networks that manage idiosyncratic risk and basis risk within communities (Takahashi *et al.* 2019). Second, with the government as the sole policyholder/purchaser, many challenges with respect to financial literacy and trust can be overcome at a lower cost. ARC also provides comprehensive capacity-building services to clients, which is done much more easily for such a centralized macro product than for a spatially dispersed micro program. Third, macro and modified macro products require less product distribution infrastructure than micro-level programs, being focused on a single policyholder. Costs for onward distribution to shock-affected individuals remain, however, and can be significant, for example, in the form of household targeting and registration needs (Fava *et al.* 2021).

Macro-level insurance programs, including IBLI, can also prove worthwhile to governments and nongovernmental organizations (NGOs) from a financial management perspective (Barrett & Maxwell 2007). When stochastic events (like droughts in pastoralist regions) create stochastic budgetary liabilities for governments and NGOs, insurance can offer a more effective means to pre-arrange the needed response funding compared to other budgetary tools such as reallocations, international borrowing, and fundraising appeals (Clarke *et al.* 2017; Carter *et al.* 2021).

The economic logic of index insurance as a response to insurance market failures in low-income agrarian settings has motivated a wide range of donor- and government-funded interventions throughout the world over the past ten to twenty years (Carter *et al.* 2017). The added benefit of asset insurance in settings characterized by poverty traps makes IBLI especially compelling, both as a micro-scale product targeted at individual purchasers and as a macro-level policy instrument for governments or NGOs. However, much depends on key details around product design, distribution, and an enabling policy framework, which we discuss in subsequent sections.

4 Institutional and Implementation History of IBLI

From its conception to its modern-day scale, IBLI has progressed from a commercial pilot in one Kenyan county with a single retail sales channel, to a market with several products sold across three countries through multiple sales channels with support from a variety of actors and institutional arrangements. This progression has also moved IBLI beyond the direct influence of the original research and implementation partners and has ushered in a range of changes that illustrate the opportunities and risks that come with scaling a successful pilot. In this section, the main milestones of the IBLI journey are illustrated together with the conceptual pillars supporting IBLI's operational implementation model. We highlight the systematic (and unusual) integration of a demand-responsive scientific research arm with evidence-backed and partner-led market development, which has been critical to its success and provides critical background for Sections 5–8.

Piloting

The IBLI program originated in 2007 as a research collaboration between the International Livestock Research Institute (ILRI), Cornell University, and the University of California – Davis with the objective of studying whether insurance could mitigate the negative consequences of droughts for pastoralists in the region. After several years of research, product design, and stakeholder engagement, an index insurance policy was developed for Marsabit County, Kenya. Developing a new insurance market in a remote county with little exposure to insurance required considerable investments and innovative institutional arrangements. To be successful, IBLI needed cost-effective, efficient, and trustworthy channels for providing extension services, collecting insurance premiums, and disbursing payouts to insured pastoralists (Matsaert *et al.* 2011). The resulting marketing arrangement included a single local underwriter (UAP Insurance) supported by a global reinsurer (SwissRe) and Equity Insurance Agency (EIA) the insurance agency subsidiary of Equity Bank, one of Kenya's fastest growing Banks at the time. To help the implementing partners recoup their initial investments in developing a new product whose timeline to commercial viability was not guaranteed, ILRI signed an agreement with EIA and UAP that gave them exclusive rights to sell the IBLI product for three years.

IBLI was first launched in 2010 by EIA and UAP as a purely commercial microinsurance product sold through a network of insurance agents directly to individuals. Clients could purchase insurance coverage for camels, cattle, sheep, and goats. Coverage rates for each animal type were originally set to broadly reflect their market value and there was no minimum or maximum coverage rate set, irrespective of herd size or composition. Insurance policies provided coverage for twelve months and payouts were made either through bank accounts, mobile money accounts, or in person by cash or check.

After several sales windows, evidence that IBLI coverage was having positive impacts on buyers generated interest, additional investments by donors and insurance firms, and pressure to expand IBLI beyond Marsabit County. This expansion initially proved challenging because the product used a livestock mortality index (see Section 5), which had been parameterized for Marsabit using a unique dataset of historic livestock losses that was only available in a few select areas in the region (Chantarat *et al.* 2013). The demand for geographic expansion, combined with fruitful collaborations with remote sensing experts, spurred the development of a new index that tracked relative local forage conditions, rather than predicted livestock losses, and which could be parameterized using existing global datasets, effectively allowing IBLI policies to be developed for any region. The downside to that design innovation was the index was effectively decoupled from prospective purchasers' direct losses, raising new questions about product quality.

While stakeholders were asking for geographic expansion, several factors, including the considerable costs of marketing, sales, and distribution, along with the monopoly granted to the exclusive insurance provider, resulted in several missed sales seasons by EIA in Marsabit. That experience underscored that implementation processes were as important as product quality to ensure pastoralists had new, effective drought risk management options. Those missed sales seasons precipitated an adjustment in institutional arrangements. In 2012, the exclusivity agreement with the EIA and UAP Insurance was canceled, paving the way for new commercial partners and product innovation. One such innovation was the development by Takaful Insurance of Africa (TIA) of an Islamic Sharia-compliant version of IBLI to meet the needs of the region's sizable Muslim population. Commercial partners also began to experiment with partnering with NGOs and local government agencies to reduce supply chain costs and increase demand (Mburu *et al.* 2015). Throughout this period, ILRI worked with donors to support public–private partnerships allocated public funds to subsidize product development and extension, and with technology firms to develop more cost-effective channels for customer education and last-mile product delivery.

Micro-scale (and Growing Pains)

Between 2012 and 2016, the IBLI market grew to include three new insurance firms and several new reinsurance arrangements, all while scaling outward to a total of seven arid and semiarid counties in Kenya (Johnson *et al.* 2019) and into the Borana Zone of Ethiopia. While developing policies for the new regions required parameterization of insurance policy features through a collaborative process between pastoralists, insurance firms, and researchers, the process was relatively straightforward. At the same time, it became clear that developing low-cost and effective extension and delivery channels was more challenging. IBLI products were completely new to the pastoralists, and insurance agents had the heavy burden of not only explaining the concepts of commercial insurance but also the subtleties of the index product. Also, most local insurance firms had no experience selling index insurance, or even agricultural insurance, nor had they ever worked directly with pastoral populations in remote rangelands.

Unsurprisingly, IBLI's first five years were plagued with supply-side issues, including missed sales seasons, poorly trained agents, and uninformed clients, as insurance companies worked to develop these new markets and related infrastructure. As IBLI scaled in Kenya there was considerable churn in the insurance market. The original insurance company stopped selling IBLI, two new insurance companies entered the market, and then one subsequently exited but has since reentered. These changes created gaps in product availability, inconsistent framing of the product, and changes to insurance agents and information channels. Such inconsistencies undercut the desired image of stability, transparency, and security for insurance policies and the firms behind them. Pastoralists' demand for IBLI was low and variable in this volatile period. Section 6 further discusses the difficult period from 2010 to 2015 in Kenya.

The IBLI product itself also evolved during this time. In 2012, IBLI policies transitioned from insuring against average livestock losses to insuring against local relative forage scarcity. In 2015, the policies in Kenya went through another large shift, from a product that made payments after a drought (asset replacement policy) to one that made payments during the drought (asset protection policy) (see Section 5). In principle, this shift increased the value IBLI offered clients (Jensen *et al.* 2019) and has driven much of the subsequent discourse on anticipatory climate risk financing. But the added value of receiving indemnity payments when animals are stressed by drought but can still survive if provided supplemental feed, veterinary services, and/or water depends on the availability of those goods and services for purchase using IBLI payouts. The limited markets for livestock services in East Africa's ASALs may call that value addition into question.

Aided by meso-scale purchases (discussed in the next section), the commercial sector expanded in the original markets. In Kenya alone, IBLI policies were commercially available for over 220,000 km^2 of rangelands by 2020. But pastoralists' rate of individual purchases of the commercial IBLI product remained modest

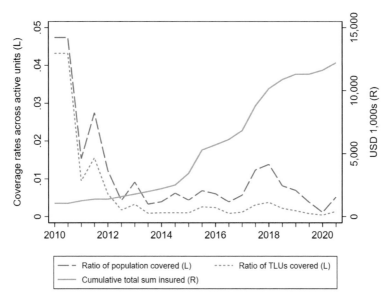

Figure 1 IBLI coverage rates of the human (long dash) and livestock (short dash) populations in active IBLI regions, both read against the left-hand axis. The right-hand axis and solid line indicate the cumulative value of the total sum insured.

Notes: Figures are for active regions in Kenya and the Borana Zone of Ethiopia only. In 2010, the active region included an area of 63,000 km^2 and a total population of less than 0.3 million individuals. By 2020, the active region included 406,000 km^2 and about 6.5 million people. The estimates of the ratio of population covered assumes 5.5 members per household. The livestock estimates do not include camels. The figure does not include insurance coverage through KLIP or SIIPE.

(Figure 1). Between 2010 and 2020, pastoralists purchased fewer than 50,000 policies, the vast majority covering two TLUs or less, insuring a cumulative value of over USD 10 million, and with renewal rates in subsequent years consistently less than 50 percent (Lung *et al.* 2021). At no point was more than five percent of the human population or two percent of livestock in regions with active IBLI availability insured through private IBLI purchases.[9] It is not clear to what extent modest individual purchase levels reflect weak demand for drought insurance generally, issues related to this specific product (e.g., product quality, price, timing of premium payments), or a continuation of the supply-side obstacles faced during the first five years.

---

[9] By comparison, livestock owners in eastern Kenya spent about USD 10 per animal to vaccinate roughly 16 percent of adult cattle against East Coast Fever, a disease that is responsible for an estimated one million cattle deaths per year (McLeod & Kristjanson 1999; Marsh *et al.* 2016).

Meso- and Macro-scale Growth

From 2010 to 2015, IBLI had only been a microinsurance product sold directly to individual pastoralists by local insurers. In 2015, the Government of Kenya added IBLI to its social protection programming by launching the KLIP, motivated in part by the logic described in Section 3. The KLIP program purchases insurance coverage for five TLU on behalf of beneficiary households, who, ideally, are targeted vulnerable households that fall just above the wealth threshold for eligibility for the Hunger Safety Net Programme (HSNP), a cash transfer program targeting the poorest households in the dryland counties of Kenya. This approach of purchasing (or heavily subsidizing) insurance for a targeted group is commonly referred to as meso-scale insurance, to distinguish it from individual purchases of insurance (micro-scale) or institutional or government purchases of insurance for themselves (macro-scale). Figure 2 illustrates the timeline of IBLI's evolution in these three scales.

KLIP initially purchased insurance on behalf of 5,000 households in two counties in northern Kenya. By 2017 it had grown to pay USD 2.4 million in premiums annually to provide coverage to 18,000 households each year for an annual total sum insured of USD 12.6 million (Fava *et al.* 2021). That is nearly equal to the total cumulative insured value through individual micro-scale IBLI

Scale	'10	'11	'12	'13	'14	'15	'16	'17	'18	'19	'20	'21	'22	'23
Micro	IBLI launched in Marsabit Kenya in 2010 and grew to include several insurance firms and to provide coverage in eight ASAL counties of Kenya. The micro product continues to be sold across northern Kenya.													
			In 2012, IBLI launched across the Borana Zone of Ethiopia and continues to be sold there by Oromia Insurance Company (OIC).											
Meso					The Government of Kenya supports KLIP, which purchases IBLI on behalf of targeted pastoralists in eight ASAL counties.								
							WFP implements SIIPE in Ethiopia, which provides conditional insurance transfers and has grown to cover 5,000 households.							
								CST launches IBLI in Dassenech Woreda, Ethiopia.					
								ICRC pilots IBLI in Meyumuluke Woreda, Ethiopia.					
								WFP pilots IBLI in Zambia.					
											World Bank's DRIVE project subsidizes IBL Iacross ASALsin Kenya, Ethiopia, Somalia, and Djibouti.		
Macro											ARC offers a rangeland customization to its sovereign product, which is based on the IBLI logic, and has been purchased by Burkina Faso, Chad, Mauritania, Niger, Senegal, Somalia, and Sudan.		

Figure 2 Timeline of IBLI scaling.

purchases of IBLI between 2010 and 2020. In part due to financial challenges associated with COVID-19, the KLIP program lapsed in 2022 and did not resume as we wrote this in April 2023.

In 2018, the World Food Programme (WFP) and the Regional Government of the Somali Region, Ethiopia, jointly launched a meso program like KLIP called Satellite Index Insurance for Pastoralists in Ethiopia (SIIPE) (Frölich *et al.* 2019). As of 2021, SIIPE provided conditional, fully subsidized insurance for a limited amount of coverage, underwritten by a coalition of local private insurance firms and reinsured through international markets, to 28,300 pastoral households in the Somali region (WFP 2021). WFP has also piloted a similar scheme in Zambia (WFP 2022).

The SIIPE program offers an example of an alternative approach to IBLI provision. Unlike comparable collaborations in northern Kenya and southern Ethiopia, the IBLI-ILRI team had only a short-term engagement with the WFP-SIIPE team, focused on product design and capacity development. WFP then led the implementation activities including the extension and sales activities, which were previously either left to insurance firms or ILRI intervention, by adding responsibilities to its existing field staff.

Three key learning points are worth highlighting. First, once the tools and processes are developed and in place users like WFP may lead such efforts with minimal backstopping from technical partners. Second, there can be large advantages to using existing field staff for the last-mile distribution processes for insurance. The marginal costs of additional extension and sales activities for field staff that are already operating in the communities are small compared to the costs of onboarding and training new insurance agents, and they may already have relationships with community members that can support their sales activities. Third, implementation divorced from technical monitoring and evaluation runs some risks as regards product quality assurance. This latter issue has become increasingly salient as IBLI scales and in the absence of effective regulation requiring a credible signal of quality (see Section 8).

Other local and international organizations have also started using IBLI in their resilience-building operations and social protection programs by subsidizing insurance premiums for drought-vulnerable pastoralists. In 2020, a joint entity of three institutions (the Catholic Agency for Overseas Development [CAFOD], the Scottish Catholic International Aid Fund [SCIAF], and Trócaire) known as CST worked in Ethiopia with ILRI and a local insurer – Oromia Insurance Company (OIC) – to develop an IBLI policy for the Dassenech *woreda* (administrative district) of South Omo. The collaborating partners provide a 70 percent premium subsidy to pastoralists in the region. The International Committee of the Red Cross (ICRC) has partnered with OIC and

ILRI to use IBLI to support long-term displaced pastoral populations in the East Hararghe Zone of Ethiopia. In January 2021, ICRC started offering an 80 percent premium subsidy to residents of the Meyumuluke *woreda* as part of its livelihood and resilience-building programming. Meeting these new project-level objectives and targeted interventions requires adaptation in how insurance products are designed, roles are allocated among stakeholders, and products are sold.

The public use of private insurance mechanisms garnered considerable interest from several governments, especially those with large pastoralist populations. In 2019, delegates from the Intergovernmental Authority on Development (IGAD) region met in Addis Ababa at the "High-Level Ministerial Policy Roundtable and Technical Workshop" to discuss the potential for regional collaboration and coordination between countries as they developed their own IBLI programs. This resulted in several donors commissioning regional feasibility studies in the IGAD region (Lung *et al.* 2021) and separately in the Sahel (Thebaud 2016; Fava *et al.* 2018). IBLI is also a major element of the World Bank-funded multicountry De-risking, Inclusion and Value Enhancement of Pastoral Economies in the Horn of Africa (DRIVE) project that was launched in 2022 (World Bank Group [WBG] 2022). The various discussions also highlighted the importance of the underlying regulatory environment and complementary risk management tools to address distinct risk layers (see Section 8). Figure 3 shows IBLI's expansion from the initial pilot in Kenya through to 2022.

While KLIP, SIIPE, and DRIVE are all examples of meso-scale programs, the IBLI contract design has also been employed by Africa Risk Capacity Limited (ARC Ltd) in a rangeland customization of its sovereign (macro) insurance product that it offers across the Sahel and East Africa.[10] The largest share of IBLI coverage has thus come through coordinated, bulk purchases under KLIP, SIIPE, and similar macro- or meso-scale programs.

The geographical and vertical expansion of the IBLI agenda, from a micro-oriented pilot in Marsabit with a single insurance firm to supporting several insurance firms and collaborating partners operating at micro-, meso- and macro- scales across multiple countries, required continuous adaptation of IBLI to accommodate unique characteristics and objectives of varying stakeholders (pastoralists, state, and non-state actors), institutions (finance, governance, etc.),

---

[10] ARC Ltd is a financial affiliate of the ARC group, a specialized agency of the African Union, established in 2012 to help African governments improve their capacities to better plan and effectively respond to extreme weather events. ARC Ltd, was founded in 2014 to provide index-based insurance focused on climate related disasters to provide ARC Group with a concrete instrument to advance its mission.

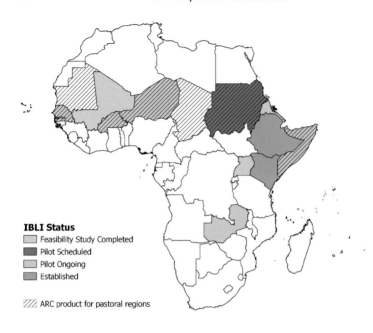

Figure 3 The diffusion of IBLI and IBLI-like products in Africa.

and infrastructure while striving to maintain quality standards. Throughout the development of the IBLI agenda over almost fifteen years, four key component areas have been central to the IBLI *modus operandi* since the program's inception. Those four components are

1. **Accurate and effective contract design:** Continuous efforts for increasing precision and value of the policies for pastoralists while supporting sustainable scale. See Section 5.
2. **Creating and serving the IBLI market:** Developing low-cost, effective methods for client and stakeholder awareness, educating for requisite capacities, and product service delivery. See Section 6.
3. **Evidence of IBLI impact, quality, and uptake:** Rigorously evaluate IBLI's impacts on households and its broader societal value and disseminate the resulting evidence. See Section 7.
4. **Policy and institutional infrastructure:** Supporting design of an enabling policy environment to facilitate appropriate public–private partnership (PPP) infrastructure for the delivery of a sustainable program. See Section 8.

While the weight of attention among these components has shifted over the years – largely in response to specific bottlenecks, or opportunities, encountered at various points along the IBLI journey – the symbiotic integration of these four elements has always been critical to uncover the optimal value from IBLI and guiding its trajectory to market and scale. The next several sections discuss each of these components in turn.

5 Accurate and Effective Contract Design

IBLI's contract design evolved over time, ultimately pioneering early trigger mechanisms to provide monetary support that can prevent livestock from dying and evolved hand-in-hand with the evolution and scaling of the product and program. This section reviews the key milestones in IBLI's design, taking into consideration both the technical development of the remotely sensed drought indicator used for the IBLI index and the insurance design framework.

The Original IBLI Design

IBLI's initial objective was to insure pastoralists against drought-related livestock losses, which were identified as the main risk to their welfare and livelihoods. The initial IBLI product was based on an index that estimated area-averaged livestock mortality rates at the end of an insurance season and provided payouts when the estimated average losses were greater than a pre-specified threshold, with the intention that the payouts could be used to "replace" lost livestock (Chantarat *et al.* 2013). This "asset replacement" contract was developed and validated using a statistical relationship between longitudinal observations of household-level herd mortality and a deviation of the satellite-derived Normalized Difference Vegetation Index (NDVI) from the long-term mean when tracked from the start of the rainy season until the end of the following dry season.

A coarse-resolution (~8 km) satellite NDVI product – based on data from the Advanced Very High Resolution Radiometer (AVHRR) onboard the US National Oceanic and Atmospheric Administration (NOAA) satellites – was selected as the most suitable predictor of drought-induced mortality because its long-term NDVI time series capture seasonal and interannual variations in rangeland vegetation health and abundance that are associated with spatiotemporal weather variability. While weather parameters, such as rainfall, are also a basis of multiple index insurance initiatives (Leblois & Quirion 2013), weather station coverage in Africa is generally sparse, and existing station data are often not easily accessible, making it hard to assess the accuracy of satellite-derived rainfall products. Moreover, summarizing rainfall amounts for a season does not account for within-season rainfall distribution that is important for vegetation development. NDVI can thus be a more direct indication of forage availability. Further, the NDVI data were freely available in near real time with nearly thirty years of continuous historical observations (i.e., AVHRR time series date back to 1981). The asset replacement contract was designed to cover the average risk for a covariate region – an insurance unit – over two consecutive insurance seasons, with an insurance season defined as a combination of the rainy season and the following dry season. Clients could purchase coverage for camels, cattle, sheep, or goats, which were then aggregated into TLU, and insurance payouts were made by multiplying the cost of replacing one TLU with the predicted area-averaged losses (Chantarat *et al.* 2013).

While the original mortality index functioned successfully, three main drawbacks emerged as interest in IBLI continued to grow. First, the quality of the statistical relationship between NDVI and livestock mortality was heavily dependent on the quality and availability of the longitudinal household-level livestock mortality data used to calibrate the model, leading to potentially high basis risk, especially if these mortality data were sparse or inaccurate. Second, the lack of robust ground data for designing the mortality contract was a major limiting factor for the geographic expansion of the coverage.[11] Third, clients and other stakeholders indicated a strong preference for a product that paid out prior to livestock loss with the goal of financing coping mechanisms to safeguard livestock and avert massive wealth loss.

The first two of these drawbacks – the need for long panels of livestock loss data and the sensitivity of product quality to errors in those household data – were addressed in 2012 when a new contract was developed that used seasonal NDVI anomalies directly as an index of forage scarcity.[12] This new contract did not rely on livestock mortality data, but rather on the well-established relationship between NDVI and the green biomass production of rangelands (Fava & Vrieling 2021). Abstracting from livestock mortality to forage scarcity was possible because, for most extensive pastoral systems, forage availability is

---

[11] The original IBLI product was designed for Marsabit District using rich, monthly household survey data collected by a government program (described in Mude *et al.* 2009). Those predictions were validated out-of-sample using two years of quarterly household survey data from the same district collected by the PARIMA project (described in McPeak *et al.* 2011). A household survey data series including high frequency, longitudinal, livestock mortality is rare. We are not aware of any similar data series from pastoral areas.

[12] Degradation of NOAA-17 AVHRR data in 2011 prompted a transition of IBLI data source to the Moderate Resolution Imaging Spectroradiometer (MODIS) sensor on the Terra platform. MODIS data were available only since 2000, but Vrieling *et al.* (2014) demonstrated the possibility to extend the AVHRR-based index with the MODIS-based index, enabling reliable continuity of the original index time series.

a fundamental determinant of livestock survival, as alternative feed resources are largely unavailable or unaffordable. The global availability of NDVI data and the independence from ground datasets allowed expanding IBLI geographic scope and prompted the launch of the product in several new areas.

The third drawback was addressed in 2015 with the development of the "asset protection" contract which modified the previous contract by anticipating the payout timing. The idea of this contract was that the insurance payouts could help pastoralists protect their livestock before they died. Whereas livestock losses principally occur in or directly following the dry season, those losses are the result of inadequate forage growth during the wet season due to below-normal rainfall. Wet-season NDVI could thus be used as an indicator of wet-season forage accumulation and therefore coming (dry-season) forage scarcity. The new early indicator of forage accumulation, coupled with the introduction of electronic payments, preceded the devastating impacts of the drought, thus providing an earlier basis for payout, and perhaps for wealth preservation (Vrieling *et al.* 2016; Fava & Vrieling 2021).

Design of the Asset Protection Contract

The asset protection contract covers the risk of a significant deficit of forage growth during the rainy season, which leads to insufficient forage to feed the livestock during the subsequent dry months. The accumulated wet season forage production is gradually depleted during the dry season through decomposition and by livestock and wildlife grazing. When droughts strike, less forage accumulates during the wet season, leading to forage deficits that cannot support livestock nutrition for the duration of the dry season. The result is that livestock die from starvation and/or become more vulnerable to fatigue, diseases, predators, and other risk events, such as heavy rains or floods at the beginning of the next wet season, unless households spend additional resources on inputs (e.g., forage, water, relocation, veterinary services). An asset protection contract can, in principle, enable households to use indemnity payments to purchase those inputs and prevent their animals from perishing. However, the effectiveness of the indemnities for herd protection depends on whether existing active markets in those inputs can respond to a surge in demand due to indemnity payments.

The NDVI processing chain to calculate the IBLI forage scarcity index for the asset protection contract includes three main steps (Vrieling *et al.* 2016). First, the NDVI data are spatially aggregated by taking the area-average NDVI per insurance unit for each (ten-day) NDVI composite. The insurance units are defined by a combination of operational criteria (i.e., administrative boundaries or natural boundaries like rivers) and local knowledge of seasonal herd mobility patterns, ethnic boundaries to traditional grazing ranges, and local agroecology. The approach followed for IBLI starts from the lowest level of mapped administrative units and works with local communities and institutions to combine or adapt these to define meaningful and clearly delineated insurance units, masking out non-rangeland areas such as impervious surfaces, and large bodies of water (Chelanga *et al.* 2017).

Second, NDVI time series are temporally aggregated during the season to derive a seasonal index. Defining the start and end period of aggregation can be guided by expert knowledge of rainfall/vegetation seasonality or by analysis of the satellite-derived temporal NDVI profiles (Vrieling *et al.* 2016). Finally, the aggregated seasonal NDVI is normalized to obtain an index that indicates how the seasonal forage compares to season- and unit-specific forage conditions during the past fifteen to twenty years (i.e., the full length of the data time series). There are several approaches for normalizing the aggregated season NDVI values, for example, z-scoring (subtract mean and divide by standard deviation), linear scaling between the minimum and maximum historic values (i.e., the vegetation condition index [VCI]), or percentile calculation. When a pre-defined index threshold value is reached,[13] payouts are made proportionally to the severity of the forage deficit. The indemnity is calculated as a fraction of the total sum insured, corresponding to the estimated cost of keeping one TLU alive.

Asset protection contracts are currently provided by several private firms and programs in Eastern and Southern Africa (see Fava *et al.* 2020; Lung *et al.* 2021; Section 4 for an overview). While the backbone of the design is the same for all the products, differences in the purpose among the various drought risk financing schemes (i.e., microinsurance, modified macro social protection, sovereign-level insurance) have led to several customizations of the parameters and to adaptations of the design and risk layering approaches.

Innovating IBLI Product Design

Progress in Earth observation technologies and applications creates new opportunities to support drought index-insurance (Benami & Carter 2021; Fava & Vrieling 2021; Vroege *et al.* 2021), while anticipatory risk financing is increasingly promoted as a key part of climate adaptation strategies in low-income economies (Weingärtner & Wilkinson 2019). While the most significant

---

[13] For IBLI, typically the trigger (i.e., the threshold index value below which the index triggers payouts) has been set as the 20th percentile of the index empirical distribution function. The exit (i.e., the threshold index value below which the maximum payout is triggered) has been set with different approaches over time.

transition in the IBLI design was from predicted herd mortality to forage scarcity contracts and from asset replacement to asset protection contracts, the index design has evolved continuously in response to research findings and stakeholder feedback (Fava & Vrieling 2021). This section summarizes the key challenges, lessons learned, and future opportunities, both in terms of the technologies supporting index design and in terms of the broader insurance product design framework.

Advances in the Biophysical Index

IBLI's forage scarcity index is a measure of relative seasonal vegetation activity, and as such provides an indication of reduced forage development in specific seasons due to drought (Fava & Vrieling 2021). Nonetheless, many alternative drought indices exist (West *et al.* 2019) derived from precipitation, soil moisture, or evapotranspiration data products. In recent years, the accuracy of such products has improved, in part, due to sensor improvements (Vroege *et al.* 2021). While the link between these products and forage availability may be less direct, they could potentially benefit IBLI in several ways. First, given that green vegetation abundance is not solely a function of water availability and can be influenced also by non-palatable green vegetation, products that accurately describe different aspects of the water cycle may be used to calibrate the forage index to single out drought-induced reductions of forage (Enenkel *et al.* 2019). Second, because of the time lag between drought stress and its effects on vegetation (Udelhoven *et al.* 2009), these products may allow for earlier identification of drought, possibly facilitating earlier payments. Initiatives such as the "Next Generation Drought Index" project (Osgood & Enenkel 2020) aim to bring multiple drought indices together in a toolbox for optimal selection against drought impact data, such as crop yields or rangelands herbaceous biomass.

Most index insurance programs that use vegetation index data, including IBLI, rely on NDVI satellite observations with 250 m or coarser resolutions. This is because consistent and frequent observations throughout the season over many (e.g., more than ten) years are needed to effectively capture the effect of climate variability on seasonal biomass production. Particularly cloud cover reduces the number of useful satellite observations in certain seasons, which can partially be overcome with daily, or close to daily, revisit capability, thus offering more possibilities for cloud-free observations. In recent years, other satellite missions have been launched that combine high spatial resolution with relatively short revisit times. Examples are the 10 m-resolution Sentinel-2 twin satellites and the 3 m-resolution fleet of 150+ PlanetScope satellites, both providing valuable insights into rangeland dynamics (Cheng *et al.* 2020). Despite these time series' being limited to a few years (e.g., Sentinel-2 starts in 2015), continuous delivery into the future would eventually provide time series similar in length to those currently available from the Moderate Resolution Imaging Spectroradiometer (MODIS). While the spatial IBLI insurance units are expected to remain large because of the nature of herd movement within transhumant pastoralism, starting from smaller grid cells may help to focus the insurance index more precisely on areas that are most relevant for forage production. These higher-resolution data could already provide a useful input for creating better rangeland masks, for example by discarding areas deemed unsuitable for forage provision, such as areas where non-palatable invasive species like *Prosopis juliflora* dominate (Meroni *et al.* 2017).

Other approaches for processing NDVI time series exist, which have the potential to increase the accuracy in tracking the risks that pastoralists face. For example, De Oto *et al.* (2019) aimed to better account for ecological variability within insurance units by grouping grid cells with similar NDVI trajectories using unsupervised classification techniques. This clustering can identify more uniform and ecologically meaningful insurance units, even if pastoral practices typically make use of a wider landscape for animal grazing, with land covers of different characteristics. The grouped grid cells within a single cluster then define the distribution of seasonal NDVI within that cluster. In this way, the anomaly (z-score) is not merely derived from a unit-level time series of fifteen to twenty years, but from the time series of all pixels with similar temporal behavior, improving the statistical basis of assessing anomalies. This approach allows to map pixel-level anomalies, which can subsequently be aggregated to spatial insurance units, for example, by assessing the percentage of grid cells within the insurance unit that have a z-score below a specific threshold (e.g., -1.0). Another example of improving spatial aggregation could be through the delineation of insurance units based on seasonal patterns of livestock distribution. In that regard, the detection of night-time livestock enclosures with high-resolution imagery (Vrieling *et al.* 2022) could help to inform livestock distribution mapping and monitoring in pastoral drylands.

Temporal aggregation is another critical step in IBLI index design. Until present, IBLI products have used a fixed start and end date for the seasonal index calculations across all spatial insurance units based on general seasonal patterns and stakeholder recommendations (Chelanga *et al.* 2017). This approach has obvious practical advantages in homogenizing sales and payout periods but can also reduce the accuracy of the index when seasonality has strong spatial and temporal variability (e.g., in case of large shifts at the start or end of the season). Vrieling *et al.* (2016) proposed using phenological analysis from NDVI time series to better define the average start and end date for each rainy season at the insurance unit level. The unit-specific season definitions could be used for temporal NDVI aggregation. That same study also assessed if the interannual variability of the forage scarcity index could be explained earlier in the season by shortening the temporal aggregation period, enabling earlier indemnity payments when conditions are poor. While results varied across insurance units and seasons, the seasonal index and consequent payout could be brought forward by one and a half up to four months with respect to the original IBLI index windows. Unit-specific phenological analyses are not currently used in actual IBLI implementation, which highlights the important tradeoffs that are implicitly being made between index accuracy, synchronized seasonality (for operational simplicity), and timeliness. Temporal aggregation remains a critical area of research for IBLI design, especially considering scaling to new regions, the increasing variability of seasonal rainfall patterns and extreme weather, and the rapid land use transition occurring in African drylands (Abel *et al.* 2021; Nidumolu *et al.* 2022).

Operational Implementation of the Contract Design

For a biophysical index to be useful in index insurance operational design, it needs to meet various requirements (Vrieling *et al.* 2014):

- **Have a strong correlation with the risk that is being insured** (e.g., livestock mortality and forage reduction). This directly relates to the need for a strong correlation to reduce basis risk and to ensure that payouts are made when and to whom they are required.
- **Be based on transparent, non-manipulable data sources and processing methods so that payment decisions can be trusted and verified easily by others**. This is important to build an understanding of and trust in the product by all stakeholders. While not all stakeholders have the geospatial and programming skills to generate insurance indices from scratch, payment decisions can be contested and thus need to be verifiable. This has been an important motivation for IBLI's reliance on freely accessible remote sensing data sources, allowing different parties to both take and verify the role of a "calculating agent." Many geospatial companies offer services to insurance schemes, but transparency is compromised if their solutions are based on proprietary data sources or processes.
- **The data source is available for a sufficiently long period to accurately represent low-probability climatic events like droughts and thereby allow for accurate premium pricing**. Although NDVI is a simple spectral index that can be calculated from any sensor measuring red and near-infrared spectral wavelengths, illumination conditions, viewing geometry, gradual

sensor deterioration, orbital changes, and preprocessing of the recorded
radiance data all affect the NDVI value assigned to a pixel. For insurance
purposes, one wants to minimize such effects unrelated to vegetation
changes, alternatively facing the risk that derived anomalies may be an
artifact of confounding conditions. Consistent data now exist from a single
sensor flown on different satellites (Pinzón & Tucker 2014; Xiao *et al.* 2017)
or from intercalibrated data acquired from different sensors (Swinnen &
Veroustraete 2008), including an intercalibration performed for the (old)
IBLI index (Vrieling *et al.* 2014). Even with a high correlation between the
NDVI of different sources, however, it is not straightforward to integrate
various sensors in building a record consistent in both average NDVI levels
and in its intertemporal characteristics. For this reason, from 2014 to 2022
IBLI relied on a single source, the NDVI derived from the MODIS instrument. MODIS had the advantage of a long series with consistent observations
from 2000 (on Terra satellite) and 2002 (Aqua) onward. At the time of writing
(June 2023) the MODIS sensor on Aqua has deteriorated to an extent that
requires shifting to a different sensor or intercalibrated dataset soon.

• **The data source should be available in near real time to allow timely
seasonal index calculations and indemnity payment.** Near real-time
imagery availability is needed to quickly announce and distribute payouts at
the end of the season. The main constraint here is the degree of data processing
required, given the primary data source. IBLI has long used the eMODIS
NDVI product distributed by the Famine Early Warning Systems Network
(FEWS NET), which was available as a ten-day composite product but comes
with an approximate three-week delay due to the temporal filtering algorithm.
Although more promptly available MODIS products exist, these are not yet
filtered, meaning that cloud and other atmospheric influences will affect the
NDVI readings (i.e., the NDVI does not always effectively represent real
vegetation conditions on the ground). One needs to consider these tradeoffs
carefully, assessing the importance of "near real time" availability.
Nonetheless, filtering or "smoothing" is an important step in the analysis of
NDVI time series to reduce noise and missing observations due to persisting
cloud effects in the composites (Atzberger & Eilers 2011).

• **The data source can be reliably delivered into the future to ensure that
contractual obligations of sold policies can be met.** This calls for back-up
solutions, particularly if the data source relies on one or a small number of
satellite sensors that could fail or further degrade in the future. The IBLI
program experienced this problem with the NOAA-17 AVHRR sensor at the
very early stages of implementation and switched then to MODIS. But MODIS
degradation has been a growing concern for some time (Wang *et al.* 2012).

Other than AVHRR and MODIS, no single sensor is presently available that can offer long-term (>fifteen years) NDVI time series. Alternative datasets require combining data from different sensors, which is a nontrivial task. Possible alternative long-term (>fifteen years) series include the combination of MODIS with Suomi-NPP VIIRS data (Skakun *et al.* 2018) or the Copernicus NDVI product,[14] which is based on various satellites (SPOT VEGETATION, Proba-V, and Sentinel-3 OLCI). These products underwent rigorous intercalibration, although concerns remain about their long-term consistency.

Improving the Insurance Design Framework

The shift toward the asset protection contract was driven largely by feedback from pastoral communities reporting difficulties in restocking after major droughts and indicating that support of their coping strategies during drought by earlier payouts would be more effective. An additional benefit of the asset protection contract is that it reduced the IBLI premium because the insured sum relates to the cost of protecting livestock, not the higher cost of replacing animals. Finally, asset protection could be linked to complementary interventions that facilitate access to feed or water resources during drought, while livestock availability for replacement after major droughts is a major challenge.

The IBLI asset protection contract was developed using anticipatory design principles, which are increasingly recognized as a valuable and cost-effective approach for mitigating the impacts of drought crises (Nobre *et al.* 2019). In this context, forecasting tools are of great interest, for instance, those using global weather modeling and/or machine learning techniques to forecast drought (Adede *et al.* 2019; Barrett *et al.* 2020b). While forecasting is not explicitly used in the current IBLI design, the choice of anomalies in biomass accumulation as a drought indicator was made to provide an early detection of coming forage scarcity and therefore subsequent impacts on livestock and livelihoods (Vrieling *et al.* 2016; Jensen *et al.* 2019).

Although the IBLI forage scarcity contract allows for much earlier indemnity payments than the mortality contract did, challenges remain due to a potential mismatch between drought-related forage-deficit timing and the seasonality of risk assumed by the policy. For example, delays in rainy season onset can extend the period of dry conditions and forage availability will remain low. This is a critical challenge for pastoralists as they have limited options to cope when

---

[14] https://land.copernicus.eu/global/products/ndvi

livestock are already stressed. Contract design options to address this challenge include the introduction of payout early in the wet season if initial rains of that season lag, which could be used as an advance of the main payout (this option has been used by the SIIPE program in Ethiopia). Alternatively, forecasting methods could be used to assess the likelihood that the seasonal index will fall below the trigger (Meroni *et al.* 2014) and a payout could be associated with a pre-defined probability threshold for a severe forage deficit. However, multiple payouts in the season can be challenging to communicate, recalling the challenges mentioned in Section 4, and operationally expensive if the payment system is not fully automated. Therefore, careful evaluation is needed to ascertain that the benefits of these more complicated policies, which may also require higher premiums, are not too small to justify their costs.

The covariate and, at times, cyclical nature of drought shocks has led to large consecutive payouts in Kenya and southern Ethiopia, with occasional severe losses for insurance companies (Fava *et al.* 2021; Lung *et al.* 2021). During periods of consecutive drought seasons, reinsurers and insurers have requested to revise the contract parameters and premium rates to reduce the total payout amounts, limiting their risk of further severe monetary losses in the short term. However, these requests have been mostly based on practical/business considerations from the private sector rather than on robust risk assessment methods. The approach currently used in IBLI for risk modeling uses unit-level empirical distributions of historical index values and percentile thresholds (Lung *et al.* 2021), making it not particularly robust because of the limited dimensionality of the time series (i.e., about twenty observations for each unit currently) and because it does not account for climate projections. Therefore, scope exists to develop more robust methodologies for determining payout thresholds and for characterizing the risk profile for each insurance unit, for example using not only historic realizations of the index but also future climate projections.

The potential impact of climate and environmental trends (e.g., changes in drought frequency and seasonality, land degradation, etc.), as well as potential cyclical drought dynamics (i.e., climatic oscillation), are not taken into direct account in the IBLI risk profiling, while they can directly and indirectly affect several fundamental aspects of contract design, such as risk modeling, index spatial (e.g., shifting herding practices, spreading of not-palatable species) and temporal (e.g., risk period) aggregation, premium pure rates (e.g., increase of costs of feed and water) and commercial loadings (e.g., for risk of catastrophic losses). For example, if forage conditions show trends within an insurance unit, using the historic distribution without accounting for those trends as a benchmark for the anomaly assessment could bias the estimated probability of the event. At the same time, any trend correction relies on some assumed parametric structure of the underlying dynamics, which is itself difficult to estimate without bias, resulting in a biased trend-corrected series. For that reason, accurately incorporating climate change impacts in product design and pricing remains an open challenge.

Apart from technical improvements in risk profiling, a complementary strategy for the private sector to mitigate their risk of catastrophic losses due to IBLI payouts could comprise geographic scaling for risk diversification and the establishment of multi-year insurance contracts. For example, the historical spatial distribution of drought events could be analyzed to evaluate how the risk of large and ubiquitous payouts would change in response to the area coverage of an IBLI program and to adjust the insurance premiums accordingly. Similarly, the adoption of longer-term contracts (especially for macro- or sovereign-level programs) may reduce the impact of adverse selection. The 2009–2011, 2016–2017, and 2021–2023 droughts suggest a cyclical behavior of severe drought episodes in East Africa, possibly associated with cyclical climatic phenomena (such as the ENSO). If pastoralist communities or governments adjust their subjective assessments of drought risk in response to such cycles – or other signals, like traditional climate forecasts (Luseno *et al.* 2003) – this raises the possibility of adverse selection. That is, demand might vary based on factors that are not considered in the current product design and pricing, but that could be correlated with the likelihood of payout. This has large practical implications for contract management and uptake. For example, the launch of KLIP during a drought cycle resulted in large payouts, and severe losses for the underwriter and reinsurer, which led to increases in the premium rates subsequently demanded by insurers looking to recoup their initial losses. At the same time, other programs have launched during non-drought cycles, which has led to a lack of payouts and difficulty in building confidence among pastoralists about IBLI's value. Pastoralists demonstrably exhibit buyer's remorse after a policy lapses without payout (Tafere *et al.* 2019).

Quality Assurance

During the IBLI piloting stage (2010–2015) a robust impact assessment framework was put in place with regular household surveys and randomized control trials supporting contract adaptation and generating evidence on the quality, value, and impact of the product. This evidence motivated the launch of scaled KLIP and SIIPE programs.

A rigorous basis risk assessment of the asset protection IBLI contract – as distinct from the asset replacement contract evaluated in Jensen *et al.* (2016) – has never been conducted, and no significant investments have been made to support robust data collection for product design evaluation or for impact assessment since the pilot period. Despite the increase in size and economic relevance of the program, as well as the growing availability of satellite data products and index-based insurance solutions offered by private companies, investments in contract quality assessment, contract revision and customization, product comparison, and minimum quality standards have not kept pace. This mismatch underlines the urgent need for investments in regular data collection to support contract design evaluation, and for the establishment of formal standardized quality assessment processes (i.e., certification).

Robust ground data collection remains a key constraint to improving and scaling IBLI across African drylands and should be considered a key component of ongoing and future programs. The lack of sufficient and high-quality ground data on drought outcomes is a major constraint for rigorous assessment of product performance and for testing new solutions (Osgood *et al.* 2018). Potential data sources include multi-year forage biomass measurements (Roumiguié *et al.* 2017), drought recall exercises (Osgood *et al.* 2018), and longitudinal household surveys on drought outcomes such as livestock mortality (Jensen *et al.* 2019), forage availability, or child nutrition (Mude *et al.* 2009). The high cost of collecting such data effectively precludes sustained efforts in this direction. Ground-based digital technologies and smartphone-based approaches can provide new opportunities to address this challenge. A good example is the repetitive observation of the same vegetation, either by permanent cameras (Inoue *et al.* 2015; Browning *et al.* 2019) or through pictures acquired by mobile-based micro-tasking or crowdsourcing platforms (Chelanga *et al.* 2022). Picture-based approaches for forage or livestock body condition assessment techniques (Alvarez *et al.* 2018; Liu *et al.* 2020) could also be used to support audits in case of basis risk events and to develop innovative insurance products integrating satellite and ground data (Ceballos *et al.* 2019).

On standardized quality assessment processes, there has been some progress, such as the theory-based approach of Jensen *et al.* (2019) and the USAID-funded Quality Index Insurance Certification (QUIIC) initiative to introduce minimum quality standards through a formal certification process (Carter & Chiu 2018a), which are discussed more in depth in Sections 4 and 8.

Moving Forward

Despite considerable research and successful innovation in product development so far, several open questions remain regarding IBLI product design, especially with respect to geographic scaling. No substantial modifications have been made to the operational asset protection contract since it was introduced in 2015. While this may reflect the overall effectiveness of the design, we believe that it also indicates that trade-offs and long incubation periods exist when introducing substantial changes for large operational programs. In addition, the identification of potentially improved indices and contract designs has been hampered by the difficulty in quantitatively assessing potential candidates because robust datasets and methods to assess alternatives remain lacking.

Critical research priorities for product design include the identification and testing of new long-term vegetation datasets and strategies to guarantee continuity of data provision, the development of shared and transparent quality assessment approaches, the establishment of data collection networks for contract performance assessment and monitoring, and the development of new strategies to address risk profiling challenges associated with increased climatic variability and environmental trends. Product design has been a critical pillar for the development of IBLI and should remain so in the scaling phase, which would require a continuous adaptation of the contract design and its operational implementation to meet the specific needs of IBLI programs.

6 Creating and Serving the IBLI Market

For IBLI to move from a promising concept to a concrete solution, it needed to build a coalition of supporters, ensure compliance with national regulations, and develop a new insurance market. Efforts to identify initial market partners (EIA, UAP Insurance, and SwissRe) and to win the endorsement of key public gatekeepers – for example, government technical ministries, local elected representatives, insurance regulators, the Supreme Council of Kenyan Muslims – were aided by the credibility of the research process and partners (initially comprised of ILRI, Cornell University, the University of California at Davis, and Kenya Agricultural Research Institute). Early research outputs studying the initial IBLI contract design, simulated impact assessments and willingness to pay, as well as analysis of the institutional and policy environment that could guide the design of the pilot also provided further anchoring around which key stakeholders could rally (Chantarat *et al.* 2007; Chantarat *et al.* 2008; Mude *et al.* 2009; McPeak *et al.* 2010; Matsaert *et al.* 2011; Ouma *et al.* 2011). But IBLI was an unconventional product to regulators and underwriters. Further, the target population often lived remotely far outside existing insurance sales channels, was largely unbanked and unfamiliar with insurance, and was poorly served by communications and transport, making product promotion and delivery difficult and expensive. Meeting these challenges required experimentation, institutional innovation, considerable capacity development at many levels, and policy change; all activities that remain critical as IBLI expands today.

Challenges to Market Development

IBLI's first four pilot seasons (2010–2011) signaled the credibility and value of the IBLI product. A severe drought caused a humanitarian crisis in the region and received widespread media coverage in 2011, some of which explained and highlighted the IBLI concept and covered IBLI payout events as the product performed as designed. This led to greater interest from key stakeholders, including insurance companies, NGOs, and donors, which, in 2012, then enabled the extension of IBLI to other counties in northern Kenya and into southern Ethiopia. The pilot period also offered important insights into the key challenges that would need to be solved to place IBLI on a solid trajectory for sustainable scaling.

Key obstacles to widespread adoption included (1) weak transport and communications throughout this region, especially in the pilot period, before cell phone service became reasonably widespread and reliable; (2) challenges and costs of developing and maintaining networks of agents to provide marketing and sales; and (3) costs related to the process of making indemnity payouts, such as locating clients and hiring security. The complex and costly logistics of customer acquisition and retention were also the principal driver of initial churning among commercial underwriters.

Generally, low uptake and limited repeat purchases outside research-supported sites signaled the challenge of establishing informed effective demand. This led to waning interest from the initial commercial partners (Banerjee *et al.* 2019; Johnson *et al.* 2019). Concern for reputational damage resulting from gaps in implementation, misunderstanding of the contract by client pastoralists, and poor communication clearly highlighted that sustaining, much less scaling, IBLI would require greater investment in client and stakeholder engagement.

The considerable cost of making IBLI available and supplying complementary extension to build client awareness in the remote rangelands challenged the argument that index insurance offered lower implementation costs over conventional insurance products. Finding innovative solutions to reduce those costs became a key focus for IBLI's stakeholders. This meant understanding the channels of information flow (receiving and providing) and the existing formal and informal network systems of the pastoral community. In addition, leveraging nascent but growing digital and mobile solutions became important for supply chain management, financial intermediation, customer acquisition and management, awareness creation, as well as index verification and payout announcement (Dror *et al.* 2015; Wandera *et al.* 2015; Banerjee, Khalai *et al.* 2017; Mude 2017).

Digital and mobile innovations offered only a partial solution. The small scale of the pilots also posed a challenge, given the considerable fixed costs that IBLI implementation entailed. Until this point, a coalition of researchers had been coordinating the IBLI agenda through its influence over the pilot operations. For IBLI to scale it became necessary to identify and catalyze a broader consortium of strategic partners, and to support the development of innovations and capacities that would incentivize organizations to invest in scaling IBLI to increase alignment with their own organizational objectives.

Setting Up IBLI to Scale

To support the emergence of a viable market for the delivery of IBLI and catalyze the development of capacities required for effective provision, the IBLI research team at ILRI which was the lead research institution in the IBLI consortium and had been coordinating many of the activities related to IBLI, had to expand its agenda beyond a typical research program. In 2012, it lobbied ILRI management to approve the establishment of a Market and Capacity Development (MCD) unit within ILRI to support IBLI. The unit was nontraditionally staffed by personnel with the private sector or development agency experience, serving as the connective tissue between the more traditional researchers working on technical issues of product design and impact evaluation, and the community of clients, service providers, and policy makers who were equally critical to IBLI's sustainability and scaling.

The MCD unit played a critical role as an innovation catalyst, supporting private sector partners, often with the support of local NGOs, to identify and test out innovations for more efficient service delivery, and serving as knowledge advocates rallying policy makers and development partners to invest in support of an enabling environment for IBLI. Scaling the product required not only adapting it for new locations, but also supporting the insurance companies by working with them to identify and find solutions to the challenges of selling IBLI. For example, low capacity and poor supervision (due to remoteness) were identified as a hindrance to client understanding and a potential risk for theft of collected premiums or payouts to be made. The research and MCD teams worked with insurance providers to develop a set of digital tools including agent training tools to remind agents of key product features; digital job aids that standardized the information that prospective clients received; and a sales platform to improve efficiency in the client registration process while minimizing the potential mismanagement of clients and their premiums by the agents (Wandera *et al.* 2015; St. Claire & Banerjee 2019; Taye & Jensen 2019).

While the digital tools addressed some challenges, the low density of clients combined with a costly, ineffective, and ultimately unsustainable agent model. As insurers initially maintained IBLI agents only through the two selling windows prior to the start of each rainy season, this periodicity of employment resulted in high turnover among agents. At the same time, low literacy and numeracy rates in the target regions made it extremely challenging to identify and recruit appropriate sales agents. This was a significant demoralizer for the insurance companies, especially in Kenya (Banerjee, Khalai *et al.* 2017). This led the insurance companies to request the MCD unit and researchers to study and innovate alternative agent models. The main suggestion, to use shop owners as insurance agents because they are trusted, have demonstrated basic book-keeping capability, engage regularly with many potential clients, and already have a stable income, was adopted, and is still used today. A second suggestion, to target urban professional dwellers who could purchase the product on behalf of family members residing in the rural areas (Banerjee, Mude *et al.* 2017; Hammonds & Banerjee 2018), was added to TIA's implementation strategy.

Growing interest from the Government of Kenya and demands from the beneficiaries to address some of the technical challenges of the contract, resulted in a change of the parameters of the contract from asset replacement to asset protection (Banerjee *et al.* 2022). This was significant not just for the technical features of the product (see Section 5), but also in that the processes led to several knock-on innovations. One such innovation was a digital tool that could be used to look up and display the history of index values for any insurance unit from 2002 to the present day. This tool was used to show pastoralists when the product would have historically paid out to insured clients so that those prospective clients could better understand the product and if it accurately covered the risks that they faced. This was also part of a new process that relied more heavily on community input for delineating the boundaries of the insurance units so that they could better reflect migration patterns (Chelanga *et al.* 2017).

The approach adopted by the team of researchers and MCD specialists dem-onstrated the importance of systematic and iterative interplay between IBLI's "Science Platform" that deployed rigorous analysis, and its "Implementation Platform" that deployed market and capacity building expertise, convened net-works, and facilitated change processes. This description both defines and con-textualizes IBLI's operating model, as intricately linked to its research and innovation agenda, ensuring both traction and legitimacy, while maximizing the chance for a user-defined solution that can appropriately scale for broad impact (Banerjee *et al.* 2019).

Key Lessons for Scaling Innovations

The concrete and productive interaction between the research and implementa-tion groups working on the IBLI agenda helped build a community of IBLI stakeholders – client pastoralists, private sector providers, implementing agencies such as local and international NGOs, government regulators and policymakers, and financial donors – who engaged actively, providing support and contributions critical to learning, product improvement, and scaling. This transdisciplinary and trans-sector approach proved critical for turning a research innovation into an intervention that addressed a development challenge at scale. As such, the experience of initiating and scaling IBLI generated several lessons that are generalizable to the process of incubating clever research ideas into impactful development innovations and shepherding them to widespread adoption.

- **Successful innovation is an iterative process that requires persistence, flexibility, and strong feedback channels:** While led by a research institute, the implementation agenda of the broader IBLI program expanded far beyond the boundaries of standard research projects. That was a huge part of its success. Iterative co-creation among researchers, implementers, and the target community is critical to effectively uncover and solve limiting programmatic and technical constraints as well as to identify and exploit opportunities. But it also requires considerable time, long-term funding, and strong and diverse channels of communication. This required large, repeated investments to facilitate engagements between stakeholders in different locations and with different backgrounds, for example, bringing researchers from abroad and policy makers out to remote pastoral regions to discuss with local communities how to improve the value of IBLI. Such feedback is expensive and requires effort, but also spans boundaries that can help align expectations and objectives.
- **Scaling innovations require a "trusted broker" with convening power:** Progressive insights from rigorous impact and contract assessments, along with regular and productive engagements with stakeholders seeking systematically to align interests, created confidence and momentum that allowed the ILRI team to access a growing pool of committed and valuable partners and to mobilize sufficient resources to continue innovating to meet evolving stakeholder needs. This positioned the ILRI team as a trusted broker whose value went beyond their own (especially research) contributions to include the relationships and networks they facilitated given their close engagement with the client community, academia, private and public stakeholders, and development partners alike. While in many cases the trusted broker may be a public entity or an NGO, it is important that they have the flexibility and authority (either formal or informal) to broker agreements and facilitate action.
- **Broad strategic capacity and nimble structures are critical for longer-term programs:** Where initially a few champions in key positions may have been enough to build momentum during the pilot, durable and adaptive long-term support that can withstand changing contexts (e.g., funding

shortages, turnover, and changes in partnerships) requires a broader consortium of dedicated and well-informed advocates. This requires building capacity, not only among core team members, but across all partners. As in the early days of IBLI, when a key insurer dropped out, it is imperative to ensure redundancies in strategic capacity, as well as to establish nimble and responsive structures that allow for mid-course adjustments, to ensure program resilience in the face of change. At the outset of a market-driven innovation, a capacity development and awareness creation strategy should be in place. This requires putting in place processes and mechanisms that can be used to assess and build the capacity of different stakeholders involved in the implementation, iterative feedback, and subsequent scaling.

7 Evidence of IBLI Impact, Quality, and Uptake of IBLI

As discussed in Section 3, index insurance can in principle have a transformational impact on pastoral and other rural households exposed to extreme weather risk that curtails their ability to invest and advance economically. Studies of agricultural index insurance have found that index insurance can induce behavioral change, for example by boosting investment in crop cultivation by as much as 20 to 30 percent (Karlan *et al.* 2014; Carter *et al.* 2017; Castaing & Gazeaud 2022). There is limited evidence of the impact that index insurance has on households' ability to cope with shocks, their economic welfare, or on the quality of the coverage provided by those products, in part because few studies observed shocks during their short time frames (Boucher *et al.* 2021). The IBLI product sold to herders in Mongolia is one important and relevant exception. Coverage from this product helped herders to smooth assets and recover from the insured shock more quickly than their uninsured peers (Bertram-Huemmer & Kraehnert 2018).

In Kenya, the January 2010 launch of IBLI was preceded by a September 2009 baseline survey of 924 households in Marsabit County. Follow-up surveys were collected from the same households yearly from 2010 to 2013, and again in 2015 and 2020. In the Borana Zone of southern Ethiopia, baseline household surveys were collected from 515 households in March 2012, and the initial IBLI sales started in August 2012. Follow-up surveys were collected from the same households in 2013, 2014, 2015, and 2022. In both pilots, randomly selected survey participants were provided with insurance premium discount coupons and/or invitations to learn more about IBLI, laying the foundation for a randomized encouragement design[15] that would use experimental variation in the distribution of

---

[15] An encouragement design is a type of randomized control trial in which no household is excluded from the intervention under study, as happens in treatment-control designs. In this case, households are randomly assigned to financial or informational inducements to adopt the

discount coupons and marketing outreach to causally identify IBLI's impacts in an otherwise-uncontrolled setting. This effort created two, rare, decade-long household panels based on a randomized, post-baseline intervention.

The randomized experiments and accompanying household data from these two datasets have been used in more than fifty peer-reviewed journal articles and in at least seven dissertations and theses.[16] The longitudinal nature and duration of those experiments have allowed the study of not only IBLI's *ex-ante* or behavioral effects but also its *ex-post* effects in the wake of shocks. In addition, these studies provide empirical evidence on the sensitivity of index insurance demand to price and knowledge, along with other factors that facilitate uptake, and on the resultant impacts of coverage on households. Finally, and rare among the studies of index insurance, empirical, on-the-ground data has informed the design of IBLI, which like all index insurance schemes, confronts the basis risk issue discussed in Section 3.

This section reviews the evidence on the impact, quality, and uptake of IBLI.

Before and After the Drought: The Impacts of IBLI

Pastoralists in the Horn of Africa face a variety of risks due to environmental, socio-economic, and institutional factors (Homewood 2008; Lind *et al.* 2020). Despite IBLI being associated with a single peril (covariate drought risk), the practices of pastoralists suggest that they integrate IBLI coverage into their strategies for responding to the multiple risks they encounter. For example, a study in Ethiopia found that households integrated insurance payouts into their broader coping strategies (Taye 2023) and, in neighboring Kenya, KLIP beneficiaries reported spending payouts on a variety of goods and services, many of which were unrelated to livestock maintenance (Taye *et al.* 2019). These observational studies suggest that the coverage provided by IBLI may have implications that extend beyond drought-related livestock replacement or survival.

Janzen and Carter (2019) note that the poverty trap theory (see Section 3) implies that in the absence of insurance, better-off households will cope with drought by selling assets to stabilize family consumption (consumption smoothing), whereas more marginal households will attempt to hold on to their few remaining livestock and consume less (asset smoothing). These observations

---

innovation. The statistical efficacy of this research approach depends on whether the inducements generate differential uptake between encouraged and non-encouraged households. In the IBLI studies, the randomized encouragement design improved uptake considerably.

[16] Many of the journal articles are documented at www.drylandinnovations.com/journal-articles and dissertations and theses at www.drylandinnovations.com/thesis-and-dissertations. Also see www.drylandinnovations.com/data.

suggest that the real-world impacts of insurance may be heterogeneous, allowing better-off households to sell fewer assets (preserving their long-term economic viability) and poorer households to maintain consumption even as they hold on to their assets. Based on survey data, IBLI payouts indeed allowed the least well-off to stabilize consumption relative to the uninsured, whereas better-off households sold fewer livestock relative to comparable uninsured households.[17] Other studies that used the IBLI encouragement design generated broadly similar findings (Jensen, Barrett *et al.* 2017; Noritomo & Takahashi 2020).

The IBLI research design also allowed analysis of the behavioral changes that occur when households have insurance protection against drought shocks. Jensen, Barrett *et al.* (2017) found that IBLI coverage increases investments in the intensification of livestock production, specifically in animal health as seen in expenditures on veterinary services, which matches results from crop index insurance studies that also show higher investments in increasing crop productivity (e.g., Karlan *et al.* 2014; Cole *et al.* 2017; Hill *et al.* 2019). Households with insurance also sell more livestock during non-drought seasons when prices are high and no longer employ "distress selling" during droughts when prices are low (Jensen, Barrett *et al.* 2017; Matsuda *et al.* 2019). The result is that IBLI coverage increased livestock productivity and household income (Jensen, Ikegami *et al.* 2017).

The impacts of IBLI extend beyond production and income (Taye 2022). IBLI coverage provided peace of mind for insured households, improved buyers' subjective well-being even without payouts (Tafere *et al.* 2019), and thereby reduced precautionary savings in the form of extra livestock holdings (Jensen, Ikegami *et al.* 2017; Matsuda *et al.* 2019) because of reduced future uncertainty. In addition, IBLI coverage crowded in informal risk-sharing among pastoralists, such as through increased gifts or lending (Takahashi *et al.* 2019), impacted household labor decisions (Sakketa & Kornher 2021), and induced a reallocation of children's time from herding to schooling (Son 2022).[18]

While IBLI's impacts on insured households are important, spillover or public good impacts may also be important, for example in relation to

---

[17] Janzen and Carter also showed that ignoring this essential impact heterogeneity leads to an incorrect understanding of the impacts of IBLI.

[18] Combining the findings from these latter two manuscripts to generate evidence on the mechanisms for the observed changes to labor decisions should be possible but is challenging without better information on how the labor variables are construct. In general, the evidence points towards a relative reallocation of labor in the household away from livestock herding in favor of child education and cropping related activities. One plausible mechanism is that IBLI coverage reduced the household's use of labor-intensive, risk-reducing herding practices that, with insurance coverage, had lower expected welfare returns than do the activities that labor was reallocated towards.

sustainable rangeland use in the IBLI study areas. Stakeholders have worried that IBLI could result in larger herds or changes in herding practices that could lead to rangeland degradation (Müller *et al.* 2017; John *et al.* 2019; Bulte & Haagsma 2021), although empirical evidence for this is lacking. Toth *et al.* (2017) found that households with IBLI coverage accumulate larger herds and graze them less extensively, which, if generalizable, is a serious concern if IBLI were to scale. In contrast, several other studies found that IBLI resulted in reduced herd sizes (Jensen, Barrett *et al.* 2017; Matsuda *et al.* 2019), likely because it reduces the need for precautionary savings in the form of livestock. The only study that directly estimates the impacts of IBLI coverage on rangeland health, for which remotely sensed observations of bare ground are used, found no adverse impacts, and if anything found mildly positive effects, likely due to reduced precautionary savings in the form of larger herds (Wilcox *et al.* 2023). While the impacts of IBLI on rangeland health remain unsettled, insurance has the potential to impact production decisions and therefore environmental conditions. Policy makers and practitioners that invest in supporting IBLI-like products should therefore set up funding and processes to monitor impacts.

Basis Risk and the Quality of Protection under IBLI

While ample evidence demonstrates IBLI's positive impacts, it is nonetheless an imperfect product offering incomplete management of catastrophic risk. The sustainability of positive impacts over the longer term depends on the reliability of IBLI to deliver payouts in those moments when households need assistance most. As discussed in Section 3, the biggest strength of index insurance – it does not need to measure nor verify individual yield losses – also generates its greatest weakness: basis risk. Basis risk is the difference between the losses experienced by an individual household and the losses indemnified by the index product and is composed of two components (Figure 4).

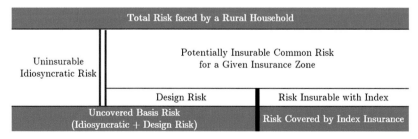

Figure 4 Why Index Insurance Contracts Fail: The Sources of Basis Risk.
Source: Based Benami & Carter (2021).

Design risk results from any differences between the index and the average losses within the insurance unit. Idiosyncratic risk arises from differences between the average losses of the insurance unit and the losses faced by an individual. Intuitively, index insurance has the greatest potential value when covariate risk comprises a large portion of an individual's risk exposure – thus idiosyncratic risk is low – and the index is accurate, meaning design risk is low.

How important is basis risk? At a theoretical level, Clarke (2016) showed that basis risk can undermine the extent to which households value and would be willing to purchase insurance. Indeed, severe basis risk may make the most risk-averse households, those that should place the highest value on insurance, the least likely to purchase such insurance. Elabed and Carter (2015) showed that the impact of basis risk on the value of, and thus demand for, index insurance may be even worse than Clarke expects if we use alternative models of household decision-making that are more informed by behavioral evidence than the workhorse "expected utility" model employed by Clarke.[19]

The original IBLI contract was designed to maximize quality and minimize basis risk. Unlike most index insurance contracts, the original IBLI contract was parameterized using longitudinal survey data on households' historic livestock losses. Out-of-sample testing using other longitudinal household survey data from the same period and place showed that the IBLI index performed well, with 94 percent overall accuracy in identifying pay versus no-pay decisions (Chantarat *et al.* 2013). The original IBLI pilot ultimately covered an average of 63 percent of the covariate risk of high-livestock-loss events, but the covariate risk is surprisingly small compared to idiosyncratic risk so that even with IBLI coverage, pastoralists still shouldered 69 percent of their original livestock mortality risk (Jensen *et al.* 2016). This highlights that while index insurance products can be a low-cost, valuable financial tool for mitigating drought risk, IBLI offers quite incomplete protection. It is an effective but imperfect financial tool.

Those and other studies have focused attention on evaluating the quality and value of index insurance contracts. Carter and Chiu (2018b), further elaborated by Kenduiywo *et al.* 2021, develop a metric of index insurance quality. Their measure gauges the degree to which the insured household would be better off with or without the insurance over the long term given the reliability of the underlying insurance index to correctly reflect household losses. Kenduiywo *et al.* (2021) revisited the IBLI contract and evaluated its qualities following the

---

[19] While we know of no work that specifically examines the ambiguity aversion of pastoralists, if some fractions are ambiguity averse, it could help explain the modest up-take rates that have been observed.

Carter and Chiu (2018b) method. Despite its basis risk imperfections, the study showed that IBLI offers long-term value to pastoralist households and in expectation improves their economic well-being. At the same time, the IBLI contract provides only 50 percent of the economic value that a perfect (but unattainable) individual indemnity insurance contract would offer. The evidence of favorable impacts with room for improvement has motivated those working on IBLI's contract to continuously adapt and improve the product (see Section 5).

Uptake

Index insurance can only create positive impacts for households that purchase it. Who buys IBLI? Among the survey households in both Kenya and Ethiopia, approximately 30 percent of the households purchased IBLI in the first year that it was available in each location, and the cumulative number increased to over 40 percent by the end of the second year and 50 percent after four years (Figure 5; Jensen *et al.* 2018; Takahashi *et al.* 2020). This is a high rate of uptake at the extensive margin relative to crop index insurance products. This underscores the relative value of insuring assets that produce a stream of income over time compared to a single-period income realization (see Section 1). IBLI uptake at the intensive margin has been less impressive, and disadoption rates have been high. Most households that purchased IBLI insured less than one-fifth of their livestock holdings and more than half of the households who purchased IBLI in the first year allowed their policies to lapse in the second

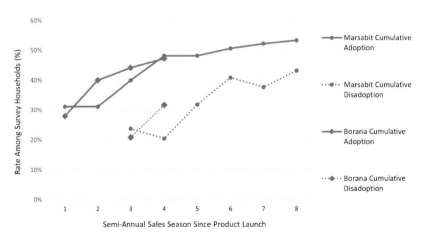

Figure 5 IBLI adoption and disadoption in Marsabit Kenya (2010–2013) and Borana Ethiopia (2012–2014) pilots.

Source: Adjusted from Jensen et al. (2015).

year. Some disadoption might reflect supply-side problems as insurers struggled to mount sales campaigns (see Section 4), but disadoption may also reflect consumer dissatisfaction.

The exogenous variation in discounted IBLI premiums arising due to the experimental encouragement design that we employed allowed the study of the sensitivity of insurance demand to price. We found that consumers were clearly price-sensitive. Estimates of the price elasticity of demand, the percent change in purchase caused by a one percent change in price, were between −0.4 and −1.2, depending on the location and circumstances (Bageant & Barrett 2017; Jensen *et al.* 2018). Concerns that premium subsidies might anchor consumers' expectation of future premium rates, thereby undermining the market later when subsidies were withdrawn, proved unfounded (Takahashi *et al.* 2016; Takahashi *et al.* 2020), which is consistent with other studies of insurance and health products (Dupas 2014; Fischer *et al.* 2019; Cai *et al.* 2020).

Unsurprisingly, contract failure events (the result of basis risk) also affected uptake. Underestimation of average losses by the index reduced subsequent uptake, and such basis risk also impacted the price elasticity of demand (Jensen *et al.* 2018). Further, those that understood the IBLI contract better, were more sensitive to these signals of product quality than those that did not understand the product well. Yet, simply improving prospective purchasers' understanding of the IBLI product did not change average rates of uptake (Takahashi *et al.* 2016).[20]

Chantarat *et al.* (2017) and Janzen *et al.* (2021) used simulation modeling, calibrated using household survey data from the region, to study the role of basis risk on demand for actuarially fair insurance in the presence of herd-size-related poverty traps. They found that pastoralists just above the poverty trap threshold (found to be 10–15 TLUs per household in the simulations contained in these two papers) would benefit more than any other group from purchasing full insurance coverage because it would protect them from shocks that could push them into the poverty trap, consistent with the social protection paradox (Section 3). But basis risk and the uncertainty that it creates lead households to invest in livestock rather than insurance to protect themselves from falling into poverty traps. Such findings have powerful implications for social programs that use IBLI (or similar insurance designs) to reduce poverty. Basis risk may reduce demand for IBLI among those who could benefit most, so targeted

---

[20] Improved product understanding may change who purchases IBLI coverage without making large changes to the average rate of uptake. Ongoing studies test if product education and purchase advice tailored to clients' own subjective assessment of risk and time preferences can improve the sorting of potential clients into purchasers and non-purchasers according to the expected value of the product.

subsidies and/or product improvements (i.e., reducing basis risk or uncertainty around basis risk) could be effective investments to realize the desired, feasible, and broader impacts to the target population.

In addition to price and basis risk, uptake also responds to environmental conditions. Pastoralists purchase insurance opportunistically, when they expect a drought (Jensen *et al.* 2018) or when vegetation conditions during the sales season are already below average (Jensen *et al.* 2018; Takahashi *et al.* 2020). Such selective purchasing is known as adverse selection and could lead to higher loss ratios for insurance firms. While insurance firms have mechanisms that they could employ to mitigate the impact of this type of adverse selection on product financial sustainability, for example, dynamic pricing conditional on rangeland conditions during the sales window, the underwriters and reinsurers involved in the various IBLI products have yet to do so, not least because of the operational complexity and potentially negative reactions from the public.

Several observational studies have explored the characteristics of those who purchase IBLI versus those who do not. For example, after conditioning for social and economic factors, there is little difference in uptake between male-headed households and female-headed households (Bageant & Barrett 2017). Further, uptake is not concentrated among livestock- or income-wealthy households, nor those with better education or larger households (Takahashi *et al.* 2016; Takahashi *et al.* 2020). One of the important questions for insurance companies' sales strategy is whether the uptake of IBLI can be influenced by other households, but there seems little social learning or peer imitation in IBLI purchase (Takahashi *et al.* 2020). While many of the implications of the diffuse nature of IBLI uptake are not yet clear, uptake patterns in the survey data do not suggest any household types suffer IBLI access limitations.

To summarize, while much has been learned about factors that shape the demand for IBLI, the fact remains that purely market-driven IBLI suffers low uptake and renewal rates that limit the product's ability to improve the well-being of pastoralist populations at scale. Indeed, individual uptake within the targeted population has been low. Only 1.5–4.1 percent of households living in IBLI regions have ever purchased IBLI since its launch, and only another 1.8 percent have received IBLI coverage through KLIP (and some of those may be in the first group as well).[21] The last mile delivery challenges faced by

---

[21] Between 2010 and 2020, 43,931 policies were sold to clients in Ethiopia and Kenya across a region with an estimated population of 5.8 million. Assuming 5.5 individuals per household, those policies would cover 4.1 percent of the population. This analysis does not account for repeat sales, which makes that estimate an upper bound. Using the maximum sales in each insurance unit across all seasons eliminates repeat purchases but also excludes many non-repeat purchases. Using this approach, the total maximum sales across insurance units sums to 16,158

private providers in sparsely populated, low-income rural areas pose a challenge, one perhaps best tackled through the aggregation of IBLI into meso- or macro-scale products (Sections 3, 6, and 8).

Moving Forward

Considerable research into the impacts and value of IBLI established strong evidence that although the IBLI product is imperfect, it generates substantial benefits for households directly by compensating households during drought and reducing catastrophic risk exposure significantly, even though incompletely (Jensen *et al.* 2016; Jensen, Ikegami *et al.* 2017; Janzen & Carter 2019; Matsuda *et al.* 2019; Tafere *et al.* 2019; Noritomo & Takahashi 2020).

Still, many questions remain unanswered. One important area of research concerns how to improve the value proposition of IBLI for both insurance firms and clients. To this end, there are several efforts aimed at reducing the cost of and increasing the efficacy of IBLI extension activities (Section 6), at ensuring that the product parameters are well synced to the impacts of droughts on pastoral households, and at improving the accuracy of the IBLI index (Section 5). Another area of research is on the potential spill-overs of IBLI coverage on broader environmental, market, and social conditions. Several micro-studies have identified individual-level behavioral changes caused by IBLI coverage but, apart from Wilcox *et al.* (2023), there has yet to be a study at the scale necessary for such inquiry. A third promising agenda examines the value that IBLI offers as a part of a safety net, social protection, or broader development programs (see Sections 4 and 8). There are good reasons to believe that IBLI could complement the development and humanitarian interventions by protecting clients from drought shocks that undermine the gains of those interventions (Jensen, Ikegami *et al.* 2017; Janzen *et al.* 2021).[22] The value and impacts of IBLI seem partly endogenous to the policy and institutional infrastructure within which it emerges. We turn now to those topics, which matter enormously to IBLI's future scaling and impacts.

---

policies, so that the lower bound figure is 1.5 percent of households have ever purchased IBLI. At its maximum, KLIP provided coverage for 18,000 households per year.

[22] For example, ongoing research explores the potential complementarities between IBLI and a poverty graduation program run by The BOMA Project, testing to see if the insurance can help protect businesses started through the graduation project from dissolving during drought (Carter *et al.* 2018). A second project examines whether IBLI could inadvertently exacerbate conflict related to drought-induced resource scarcity by increasing resource exploitation, or if it might instead mitigate such conflicts by securing needed livestock inputs during drought (Feed the Future Innovation Lab for Market, Risk & Resilience 2021).

8 Enabling Sustainable Scaling

From Incubation to Scale

IBLI's initial objective was to reduce the adverse impacts of drought-related herd losses on pastoralists in the ASALs, perhaps even to stimulate productive investments that could facilitate herders' avoidance of, or escape from, poverty traps. Early *ex ante* impact studies and empirical willingness-to-pay evidence confirmed that IBLI helped herders avoid the worst short- and long-run impacts of drought (see Section 7). Development partners and governments, who were regularly called upon to provide drought relief and struggled to balance short-run humanitarian response with long-run development objectives, saw potential value in integrating IBLI into their development and social protection toolkits. Thus began the next stage: scaling IBLI from pilot and incubation toward larger scale applications and adaptation of the product to a broader set of geographies and uses.

The initial years of IBLI were dominated by an "outscaling" process,[23] with the original IBLI product gradually adopted by a wider range of insurance and reinsurance companies and clients as it spread geographically. Critical for the acceleration of IBLI's scaling was its transition from an asset-replacement contract based on a livestock mortality index to an asset-protection contract based on a forage scarcity index (see Section 5). The shift from insuring livestock losses to insuring anomalies in rangeland greenness allowed IBLI to expand its range, supporting a greater suite of insurance products for broader climate risk management and drought response.

At the same time, this adaptation corresponded with the inability to rigorously assess the basis risk of the insurance product due to the lack of ready-to-use ground datasets of forage production and to the inherent complexity of the relationships between drought, forage scarcity, and livestock losses. For an immature technology like index insurance, de-linking the index underlying the contract from the specific loss of livestock suffered by pastoralists was consequential, especially as the technology replicates and spreads. The point is not that an asset protection product is inappropriate. Indeed, the asset protection product is based on solid theory and a more empirically generalizable method than the original asset replacement product. Rather, the point is the importance of rigorously confirming the fidelity of the index to the underlying risk against which one aims to insure.

---

[23] Outscaling is associated with the spread of an innovation within the same sphere. Upscaling refers to the creation of conducive conditions for scaling at higher levels and generally implies adaptation of the innovation for different contexts. See Hermans *et al.* (2013) and Schut *et al.* (2020) for more detailed discussions.

The launch of the KLIP was a watershed moment for IBLI. KLIP accelerated the transition from an innovation incubated largely by ILRI and its partners, to one in which a growing coalition of stakeholders, acting increasingly independently, scaled IBLI through multiple channels across multiple countries, thus to an upscaling trajectory. As KLIP launched, a broad policy review (Government of Kenya 2014) outlined the potential of public finance and policy support for agricultural insurance to protect farmers and pastoralists from climate shocks and to respond to drought-related humanitarian disasters. This further catalyzed support for upscaling IBLI to the national level and beyond. Continent-wide efforts such as the Drought Index-insurance for Resilience in the Sahel and the Horn Africa Project drew heavily on lessons learned from ten years of IBLI and provided broader evidence for scaling IBLI-based products (Lung *et al.* 2021). Regional initiatives, such as the World Bank's DRIVE project in Djibouti, Ethiopia, Kenya, and Somalia (Cerruti 2021), further illustrated the scope of interest and support for scaling this agenda.

Parallel to the growing use of IBLI products by government and multilateral agencies to protect individual pastoralists, IBLI's use also grew at the macro level as national governments began using products that were based on IBLI's principles to insure themselves against drought-related humanitarian crises. In 2018, ARC Ltd. started offering sovereign drought insurance products for rangelands based on the relative forage availability index that is used by the IBLI contract. As of 2023, those products have been taken up by several countries across the Sahel and East Africa. While the overall number of individual pastoralists directly purchasing IBLI remains modest relative to the large number of pastoralists exposed to drought risk in sub-Saharan Africa, the geographic and institutional diffusion of the IBLI approach, supported by its adoption and adaptation at multiple levels, maps out a scaling trajectory for an evolving IBLI product in Africa.

However, this upscaling trajectory poses new risks including increasingly uncoordinated actions as new actors enter the market. While the entry of new actors is critical to scaling IBLI and potentially important innovations, donors, CEOs and the projects that they support are commonly assessed by short-term business performance indicators, principally the number of clients covered. As such, insufficient attention and resources are directed toward monitoring and assuring product quality, impact evaluation, and knowledge generation for adaptive learning and course-correction, and the capacity required to support effective market development. This is despite efforts by longstanding IBLI partners to maintain those critical elements that partly account for IBLI's earlier successes. A myopic focus on sales volumes creates pressure toward unrealistic targets, potentially at the expense of longer-term development goals and of product and implementation quality. Indeed, large-scale investments in IBLI often disregard or seem unaware of hard-won lessons from the past that offer valuable insights for the development and implementation of IBLI-related programs. Hence our attempt in this Element to communicate key features that made IBLI successful in its initial, pre-upscaling stages.

Enabling Environment for Scaling IBLI

The transformational successes of agri-food system innovations are too often attributed primarily to a particular technological solution while other, often equally important, factors are frequently overlooked (Barrett *et al.* 2020a). To accurately understand, and appropriately guide, an innovation's upscaling, one must understand not only the technological innovation itself, but also the social, policy and institutional changes, and business practices that enabled transformation. Together, these are sometimes referred to as the innovation package or socio-technical bundle (Schut *et al.* 2020; Barrett *et al.* 2020a).

The difficulties encountered in recent years in upscaling IBLI highlight the need for a more holistic understanding of what made IBLI successful originally, and thus what must be preserved for it to scale into a mature, self-sustaining intervention for drought risk management. A successfully upscaled IBLI would involve public–private partnerships characterized by endogenous expansion, the widespread provisioning of insurance products supporting a growing number of pastoralist households and enterprises across different regions, while ensuring that the product remains effective, accessible, and sustainable in providing financial protection against climate risk.

In IBLI's first decade, client and stakeholder confidence in participating in its implementation was underpinned in part by rigorous research and product quality monitoring undertaken by ILRI and its academic partners and by the coordinating efforts of ILRI's incubating MCD unit, which facilitated client engagement, iterative feedback processes, and investments from critical partners. As the program transitioned from incubation to its current upscaling trajectory, several fundamental elements of IBLI's *modus operandi* (Sections 4 and 6) have weakened as the market grows beyond the capacity and influence of the original innovators that championed those elements.

A new coordinating framework – anchored through a systematic collaboration between appropriately resourced public entities vested with the relevant mandate (e.g., national governments, regulators, donors, educators) and private players incentivized by longer-horizon commercial interests – is needed at a broad scale to provide the enabling environment to support sustainable delivery of IBLI at scale. This requires intentional efforts to improve existing implementation processes and develop institutional and policy instruments consistent with the conditions conducive to supporting IBLI as a self-sustaining industry (Schut *et al.* 2020).

What mechanisms will ensure high quality, efficient IBLI contract design, and effective delivery by a growing pool of actors and leveraged by varied clients across multiple jurisdictions? And who will be responsible for tracking the impacts of these investments, ensuring product quality and value, and monitoring compliance with specified product and implementation standards, particularly when supported by public funding? What public investments are needed to crowd in sustainable private provision of IBLI or IBLI-based risk management products at scale? To offer insight, we draw from the experience and application of IBLI's program pillars (Section 4). We explore how these program pillars might adapt within an environment that enables sustainable scaling.

Accurate and effective contract design

The IBLI product design is the core technological innovation of the IBLI agenda. Several lessons can be gathered from IBLI's contract incubation stage to support scaling. During incubation, the product was gradually adapted in response to continuous interactions between researchers and a range of stakeholders, as well as rigorous research on product design innovation (Vrieling *et al.* 2014; Vrieling *et al.* 2016; de Oto *et al.* 2019; Jensen *et al.* 2019; Fava & Vrieling 2021). IBLI product quality and its effective implementation by insurance companies was facilitated by the IBLI team, ensuring frequent exchange of insights and innovation among stakeholders, and promoting co-creation that drove adoption and adaptation. Since approximately the time of the KLIP launch (i.e., 2015), no entity has played that coordinating or product quality control role. That responsibility could be devolved to national-level insurance regulators and supervisors, provided they have the technical capacity to engage in effective oversight and appropriately balance their dual responsibility to promote innovation and protect clients (Beyers *et al.* 2018; Beyers *et al.* 2020). But the lacuna around product oversight and implementation monitoring is perhaps the most obvious risk and weakness of the upscaled IBLI agenda.

The demand for product adaptation and customization that comes with scaling is increasingly driven by multiple institutions (e.g., development organizations and the private sector) with different mandates, expertise, and experience. While this is necessary and has the upside of increased technological and commercial IBLI innovation, such growth must be paired with quality assurance mechanisms and minimum standards for all products and their actual implementation (Benami & Carter 2021). Similarly, index calculation can only be carried out by a credible, independent third-party agent. Those roles could be combined, as they were in IBLI's incubation phase.

Even in relatively mature local insurance markets, index-based insurance products are novel, relatively complex, and require additional technical capacity for product design, quality control, and regulated loss-adjustment and administration. A critical mass of qualified and accessible personnel is necessary for index insurance programs to be sustainable and scalable. They must have the ability to design, evaluate, and signal the quality of an index product, which requires both actuarial and modeling expertise, as well as a well-tuned understanding of the economics of insurance and when the quality of protection offered by unavoidably imperfect index insurance is high enough to merit public support and private purchase.

Cost-effectively administering the contract requires a system of empowered and properly incentivized institutions and agents who can efficiently track the index, announce certifiable index values, guarantee transparency, announce and deliver payments in a timely manner, and provide an avenue for redress in the event of maladministration (Fava *et al.* 2018). Relatedly, reliable, and high-quality data related to the insurance contract – livestock ownership and mortality data, remotely sensed data, weather data, forage biomass, and so on – must be systematically accessible. The greater the depth of technical capacity and the sophistication and reliability of supporting institutions, the easier it is to leverage index insurance for effective climate risk management.

Effectively creating and serving the IBLI market

IBLI was designed as a market-based risk management product. While the expectation was that IBLI would eventually crowd-in private investment and spur the growth of complementary markets (e.g., for supplementary feed, veterinary inputs, and livestock) for pastoralists across the region, it was understood that there were several barriers that needed to be addressed before private investments alone could support an IBLI market. Donors and development partners initially supported considerable investments in the team of researchers working on IBLI to design the contract, evaluate its impacts, improve product distribution and administration, and incentivize increased participation by private firms.

Sustainable scaling does not eliminate the need for continuous attention to these same tasks. It just shifts the emphasis. Public resources remain critical to underwriting market development and crowding in private sector investment. As IBLI applications have diversified – to protecting vulnerable pastoralists, supporting scalable social safety nets, mitigating sovereign climate risks, and so on – the socio-economic case for deploying public resources to support scaling becomes increasingly compelling. Indeed, evidence from longstanding index-based insurance programs targeting agricultural and climate risks worldwide signal the centrality of well-structured public–private partners in driving effective upscaling (Mahul & Stutley 2010; Clarke & Lung 2015; WBG 2015)

Well-targeted public expenditures supporting IBLI provision to larger areas, can catalyze greater private-sector engagement and enhance the commercial value proposition. The marginal benefit and impact of public investments for IBLI programs will vary by the type of selected IBLI product and targeted delivery mechanism as well as by country and jurisdictional context. This, in turn, will define the optimal implementing arrangement and varied investments required by public and private players (Lung *et al.* 2021).

Commercial provision of IBLI at the micro level, particularly where clients must pay part of the premiums, remains the most complicated and costly product to deliver, particularly in remote, sparsely populated rangelands. This requires a basic level of financial infrastructure – such as a network of banks, microfinance institutions, or insurance agencies – and adequate financial literacy. Eliciting and sustaining adequate, informed demand to induce financial institutions to offer a complex product like IBLI requires public investments in ensuring client understanding and in credibly signaling product quality and value. Clients must have a clear sense of the circumstances under which they can expect to receive payouts and have confidence that the provider will expeditiously honor the contract. Such trust in the process, product, and insurer can increase over time if expectations are clearly communicated and regularly met.

Where markets are more developed and physical infrastructure such as wide mobile network coverage may facilitate more cost-effective intermediation, public investments in IBLI provisioning may prove more impactful. Mobile banking could ease client registration and the collection of requisite "know your customers" data, while efficient payment infrastructure could reduce the need to subsidize commercial delivery of IBLI at the retail scale. Where IBLI contracts support scalable safety nets delivered directly to affected beneficiaries, insurance payouts could leverage the same beneficiary registers and deployment infrastructure used for existing social protection programs or applied for disaster response.

IBLI seems more impactful where markets can provide the essential services required to cushion against the insured risk. IBLI can only protect livestock if policyholders have access to markets for animal fodder, water, and/or veterinary services and where they can use indemnity payouts to adequately provision for their drought-affected animals (Lung *et al.* 2021). Innovative bundling of IBLI with complementary products and services that increase adoption or reduce transaction costs, such as the possibility of using insured livestock as credit collateral or receiving premium discounts in exchange for localized, crowd-sourced data or reduced methane emissions from lower stocking rates, become more possible as markets expand.

Providing macro-level coverage to a sovereign client is cheaper and easier than serving individual pastoralists because insurers face fewer, more accessible clients with better access to advisory mechanisms to guide their decision-making. Even then, sovereign clients' decision-making structure, frequent turnover, and competing demands pose other challenges that require consider-able investments, especially where insurance regulatory structures or guiding policy frameworks are weak. It is also not *prima facie* obvious that it makes good economic sense for governments and other users to spend their scarce resources on indexed products. If design risk is too high these entities may be better off putting their budgets into reserve funds rather than purchasing insur-ance. Again, insurance quality matters and needs to be measured, as does the process of delivering and administering the product.

Even when national clients see the value of insurance, have secured resources, and have a supportive regulatory framework, they still must develop processes for effectively using payouts and for communicating their value to the end beneficiary and their taxpayers. While the challenge of awareness creation is more acute for commercial products targeting individuals, national clients must still be able to understand and articulate the public value of interventions supported by taxpayer resources. Furthermore, while companies might be willing to invest in marketing their product and creating brand awareness, they are not likely to invest in the public good of developing financial literacy and generalized insurance awareness. For products like IBLI that target herders in remote communities who are often on the move and commonly illiterate and unfamiliar with financial services, these costs could prohibit entry if not subsidized.

Evidence of value and impact

Public support is therefore essential to fueling growth toward a self-sustaining mature IBLI market. Maintenance and optimal deployment of public expend-itures require continued evidence of the favorable impact of IBLI programs, along with monitoring, evaluation, and learning about specific initiatives. The initial IBLI pilots were launched with robust and long-term evaluation mechan-isms integrated into their design. The resulting impact evidence (Section 7) was instrumental in generating additional resources to support IBLI's continued development and scaling. The research infrastructure also supported the evaluation and adaptation of the insurance policies (Section 5) and delivery mechanisms (Section 6), which led to improvements in service provision and product design.

While the learning from those initial research investments remains relevant, it is insufficient for the upscaling process. There is a clear and present danger presented by scaling that is not accompanied by mechanisms for long-term monitoring and up-to-date impact assessments, coupled with qualitative research geared toward adaptive learning and iterative product and program design. This danger is relevant for clients and for the reputation of those supporting the product (e.g., donors, underwriters, implementors). There are no guarantees that products or supply chains developed and proven in one context can be successfully applied to new contexts. Further, because there now exist many different stakeholders with a variety of capacities and motivations, systemic risk arises if implementation is not accompanied by rigorous, transparent, and replicable oversight. It is imperative that regulators require that those selling insurance provide evidence that their products consistently meet minimum quality standards. And if public funds subsidize IBLI-type products, the industry must likewise demonstrate that those investments generate measurable meso- and macro-level impacts.

Policy and Institutional Infrastructure to Drive Sustainable Scale

Developing and implementing a supportive policy framework, along with a regulatory regime empowering relevant institutions to enforce outlined guidelines, is therefore essential to ensure that IBLI scales effectively. The optimal mix of policies and regulations will draw from a clear understanding of the outcomes required, the key agents and institutions that must be empowered to give rise to them, and the appropriate incentives to maximize their involvement. Scaling IBLI in the market sustainably requires private sector investments to drive innovation and address market gaps by delivering value-adding services. Meanwhile, governments must invest in pre-competitive activities – for example, building financial literacy, ensuring adequate regulatory capacity, underwriting a risk layer – that benefit the entire industry and align with public objectives.

During the initial IBLI years, efforts to establish an enabling policy framework were largely opportunistic and ad hoc. IBLI was a novel innovation, and index-based insurance had no precedent within Kenya's regulatory framework. In this policy vacuum, initial efforts aimed at building strategic relationships with the key relevant institutions – national and local government, the insurance industry, technical experts, and researchers – were important to earn regulators' approval for experimentation. As IBLI matured through the pilot and incubation phase, the need emerged to transition toward more formalized public sector regulation to maintain product and service standards, to protect consumers, and to efficiently deploy public resources. However, both the capability and authority of insurance regulators and the enabling legal frameworks for index-based insurance contracts were limited, as were the mechanisms available to ensure consumer protection (Mills *et al.* 2016; Signé & Johnson 2020). This largely remains a considerable gap today, even as IBLI upscales further.

Across the globe, insurance authorities are guided by a set of core principles for insurance regulation as defined by the International Association of Insurance Supervisors in their Insurance Core Principles (ICPs) framework.[24] The ICPs aim to protect policyholders, promote fair and stable insurance markets, support innovation, and contribute to financial stability. In many countries in Africa, the ICPs are leveraged through insurance acts and guidelines which offer the supervisory regime the authority by which it defines how the insurance industry conducts business.

In Kenya, for instance, the Insurance Act (Cap 487) defines the mandate of the Insurance Regulatory Authority (IRA Kenya) to regulate, supervise, and develop the sector. It is from such a mandate that insurance industry regulators create industry-wide corporate governance regimes, such as Kenya's Corporate Governance Guidelines for Insurance and Reinsurance Companies (Insurance Regulatory Authority 2011), and provides a comprehensive schedule of industry guidelines, which are designed to provide an enabling stable environment for the insurance industry, build market awareness, and protect consumers.

Many of these guidelines set out by the IRA Kenya serve to establish the very same enabling environment that would support the sustainable scaling of IBLI. More specifically, significant steps were taken toward developing a targeted policy framework and index insurance regulations in Kenya through the development of the Kenya Index-Based Insurance Policy Paper (IRA 2015). KIIPP made recommendations meant "to create an environment that will encourage the development of the index-based insurance industry," while still providing sufficient customer protection and mapping out in detail the legal, regulatory, and design issues to consider when implementing index-based insurance schemes.

Even as the IBLI product scaled through the piloting and incubation stages, the Kenyan insurance regulator was aware of the lack of regulation of the space

---

[24] ICPs and ComFrame – International Association of Insurance Supervisors (iaisweb.org): www.iaisweb.org/activities-topics/standard-setting/icps-and-comframe/

and allowed the industry to progress without the necessary framework. This awareness of the inherent legal, regulatory, and quality risks brought about by the absence of a guiding regime may have encouraged the Kenyan government to move quickly toward the development of a supervisory regime. Beyond the KIIPP, the Government of Kenya developed draft guidelines for index insurance and revised the Insurance Act (CAP 487) to define and recognize index-based insurance. The 2015 Draft Index Insurance Guidelines, still unapproved at the time of writing in 2023, aim to provide a comprehensive regime that guides the industry from product design and pricing approval to the supervision of market conduct for insurers.

While these developments offer encouragement that insurance policy and regulation can in principle generate an effective enabling environment to support the sustainable scaling of IBLI, the best policies, and regulatory regimes are meaningless if not enacted and effectively implemented. The case of Kenya, the birthplace of IBLI, is instructive. As outlined in this Element, the first decade of IBLI was characterized by heavy investments in research on product design, impact assessment, and support to market development, and gave rise to a well-articulated policy accompanied by a clear and informed intention to develop best-practice regulation. While enacting these regulations and implementing its guidelines incentivized investments by private actors in scaling IBLI, several publicly supported large-scale programs offering a range of IBLI products in Kenya, currently operate in the absence of enforced regulatory oversight.

Meanwhile, momentum for scaling IBLI continues to grow across the region, pushed by governments' desire to protect vulnerable populations from drought. As climate risk insurance products are increasingly recognized as qualifying climate adaptation interventions, a growing pool of climate finance resources is flowing to support IBLI-like products (Scholer & Schuermans 2022; Organization for Economic Co-operation and Development [OECD] 2023). Service providers, such as the growing coalition of African insurance and reinsurance companies under the umbrella of the Nairobi Declaration of Sustainable Insurance, will orient to meet this new demand.[25] Active interest by a critical mass of primary insurers serves as an opportunity to bring IBLI-type products under the same institutional and policy regime typical of regular insurance businesses. Upon this general regulatory framework, specific guidelines for

---

[25] A declaration of commitment by African insurance industry leaders to accelerate insurance solutions in support of major sustainability challenges including climate change. Launched by the UN Environment Program's Principles for Sustainable Insurance (PSI) in Nairobi in April 2021, over 100 insurance providers had signed on by March of 2023. https://fsdafrica.org/projects/nairobi-declaration-on-sustainable-insurance/

index-based insurance products, and the various mechanisms by which they can be financed and deployed, could then be developed and/or updated.

Overall, the IBLI pilot offered a strong and evidence-based foundation on the potential value that a well-designed and implemented IBLI program can deliver to drought-vulnerable populations and the governments that serve them. As investments in IBLI scale, recalling lessons from the IBLI agenda thus far, and integrating them into product and program design can help guard against the risks of unstructured and unsupervised upscaling in the absence of clear policies and regulatory guidelines. As institutions that have the capacity and mandate to finance and support the scaling of IBLI feel pressure to accelerate the scaling of a product with proven impact, and thereby expand the provision of the drought protection that IBLI promises, they must remain vigilant to issues of product design quality and reliable implementation. Unregulated and unmonitored programs based on policies of questionable quality may lead to misinformation and/or, worse yet, real harm to poor pastoralist populations. The consequences may take years to repair, ultimately stunting, or forever halting, the provision of impactful IBLI cost-efficiently delivered at scale.

Epilogue: A New Round of IBLI Scaling Begins

IBLI continues to attract new, large investments supporting further scaling. For example, in June 2022, the World Bank approved a USD 327.5 million program (DRIVE) with the objective of helping 250,000 households in pastoralist communities in Djibouti, Ethiopia, Kenya, and Somalia adapt to climate change and better manage drought risk (WBG 2022). The project aims to crowd in more than USD 570 million in private capital to expand access to digital drought insurance and savings and connect pastoralists better to livestock value chains. IBLI is a centerpiece of DRIVE.

Significant challenges remain for the IBLI agenda and for pastoralism in the region more broadly. Many of the players in large initiatives like DRIVE are new to IBLI. Meanwhile, COVID-19 and record-high global food prices have created massive fiscal pressures on governments in the region, which affected their investments in drought risk management. Such pressures partly account for the Government of Kenya's temporary cessation of the KLIP program in 2021 and 2022. Devastating droughts continue in the region (e.g., 2021–2023) and underscore the urgency and salience of IBLI, but also leave donors and communities weary and drained of resources. They need such resources to combat other challenges confronting these same pastoralist populations, such as the spread of small arms, the rise of violent extremism, rangeland degradation, job creation for a bulging youth population, and prevention and treatment of infectious diseases.

Drought risk is just one among many threats to vulnerable ASAL populations and IBLI is just one (imperfect but potentially impactful) tool in the broader toolkit needed to improve living conditions in the region.

Following a decade of operation, will IBLI scale further and get more integrated into parallel interventions to enhance investment and livelihoods in the region? Will the leaders of ongoing and upcoming scaling initiatives maintain the close integration of research and implementation that characterized the original IBLI venture? Will such initiatives embrace the adaptive management that enables continuous improvement of a product birthed as a research effort to scale into government policy and commercial products spanning multiple countries? Will they in fact build on the early lessons of IBLI that linked contract design to the quality of insurance protection offered to clients, perhaps introducing new regulatory and, or quality certification processes? Only time will tell. The reduced engagement of insurers, reinsurers, and researchers in IBLI's promotion and product design between 2016 and 2021 may serve as a caution. We are eager to see how the myriad of lessons from the IBLI experience of the past decade-plus inform IBLI's scaling and are hopeful for its success and the renewed flourishing of the region's pastoralist communities.

The most fundamental questions surrounding IBLI's future return us to the origins of IBLI as a tool designed to facilitate escape from and avoidance of poverty traps caused by catastrophic herd losses due to drought (Section 1). Will ongoing monitoring and evaluation of the adapted and scaled IBLI product – and of its meso- and macro-level offspring – demonstrate that these investments lead to measurable escapes from and avoidance of prolonged periods of poverty? Will pastoralists covered by IBLI prove able to avoid herd loss or to restock quickly, maintain or resume extensive grazing, and recover quickly from drought shocks? What complementary risk management tools will be developed to address the various risks – for example, of conflict, disease – for which IBLI was never designed? Might some insured ASAL residents use IBLI – or its indemnity payments – to transition to or to protect livelihoods that generate an adequate, sustainable standard of living more resilient to droughts? Will the children of insured households exhibit greater educational attainment and improved health and nutrition, enabling inter-generational progress even if the current generation of adult pastoralists continues to struggle with climate shocks? How must IBLI evolve as drought risk evolves in response to climate change? As development and humanitarian organizations scale IBLI, our most fervent hope is that they remain committed to IBLI not as an end unto itself but rather as a tool to help shock-proof continuous improvement in the living conditions of some of Africa's – and the world's – poorest and most climate-vulnerable peoples.

References

Abel, C., Horion, S., Tagesson, T. *et al.* (2021). The human–environment nexus and vegetation–rainfall sensitivity in tropical drylands. *Nature Sustainability*, 4(1), 25–32.

Adede, C., Oboko, R., Wagacha, P. W., & Atzberger, C. (2019). A mixed model approach to vegetation condition prediction using artificial neural networks (ANN): Case of Kenya's operational drought monitoring. *Remote Sensing*, 11(9), 1099.

Alvarez, J. R., Arroqui, M., Mangudo, P. *et al.* (2018). Body condition estimation on cows from depth images using Convolutional Neural Networks. *Computers and Electronics in Agriculture*, 155, 12–22.

Atzberger, C. & Eilers, P. H. C. (2011). Evaluating the effectiveness of smoothing algorithms in the absence of ground reference measurements. *International Journal of Remote Sensing*, 32, 3689–3709. https://doi.org/10.1080/01431161003762405

Ayugi, B., Eresanya, E. O., Onyango, A. O. *et al.* (2022). Review of meteorological drought in Africa: Historical trends, impacts, mitigation measures, and prospects. *Pure and Applied Geophysics*, 179(4), 1365–1386. https://doi.org/10.1007/s00024-022-02988-z

Ayugi, B., Shilenje, Z. W., Babaousmail, H. *et al.* (2022). Projected changes in meteorological drought over East Africa inferred from bias-adjusted CMIP6 models. *Natural Hazards*, 113(2), 1151–1176. https://doi.org/10.1007/s11069-022-05341-8

Azariadis, C. & Stachurski, J. (2005). Poverty traps. In P. Aghion & S. N. Durlauf (Eds.), *Handbook of Economic Growth* (pp. 295–384). The Netherlands: Elsevier. https://doi.org/10.1016/S1574-0684(05)01005-1

Bageant, E. R. & Barrett, C. B. (2017). Are there gender differences in demand for index-based livestock insurance? *The Journal of Development Studies*, 53(6), 932–952.

Banerjee, R., Khalai, D., Galgallo, D., & Mude, A. G. (2017). Improving the Agency Model in Distribution of Index Based Livestock Insurance (IBLI)–A study of Takaful Insurance of Africa. *ILRI Research Report*. Nairobi: ILRI.

Banerjee, R., Mude, A., & Wandera, B. (2017). Using an Institutional History for Illuminating Project Processes and the Theory of Change: The Case of the Index-Based Livestock Insurance (IBLI) Project. IBLI practice note – ILRI and Food Systems Innovations CSIRO.

Banerjee, R., Hall, A., Mude, A., Wandera, B., & Kelly, J. (2019). Emerging research practice for impact in the CGIAR: The case of Index-Based Livestock Insurance (IBLI). *Outlook on Agriculture*, 48(3), 255–267.

Banerjee, R., Johnson, L., & Mude, A. (2022). Eliciting Pastoralist Experience for a Livestock Asset Protection Program in Arid and Semi-Arid Lands. ILRI Research Brief 113. Nairobi: ILRI.

Barnett, B. J., Barrett, C. B., & Skees, J. R. (2008). Poverty traps and index-based risk transfer products. *World Development*, 36(10), 1766–1785.

Barrett, C. B., Benton, T., Fanzo, J. *et al.* (2020a). *Socio-technical Innovation Bundles for Agri-food Systems Transformation*, Report of the International Expert Panel on Innovations to Build Sustainable, Equitable, Inclusive Food Value Chains. Ithaca, NY, and London: Cornell Atkinson Center for Sustainability and Springer Nature.

Barrett, A. B., Duivenvoorden, S., Salakpi, E. E. *et al.* (2020b). Forecasting vegetation condition for drought early warning systems in pastoral communities in Kenya. *Remote Sensing of Environment*, 248, 111886.

Barrett, C. B. & Maxwell, D. (2007). *Food Aid after Fifty Years: Recasting Its Role*. London: Routledge.

Barrett, C. B. & Santos, P. (2014). The impact of changing rainfall variability on resource-dependent wealth dynamics. *Ecological Economics*, 105, 48–54.

Barrett, C. B. & Swallow, B. M. (2006). Fractal poverty traps. *World Development*, 34(1), 1–15.

Barrett, C. B., Smith, K., & Box, P. (2001). Not necessarily in the same boat: Heterogeneous risk assessment among East African pastoralists. *Journal of Development Studies*, 37(5), 1–30.

Barrett, C. B., Chabari, F., Bailey, D., Little, P. D., & Coppock, D. L. (2003). Livestock pricing in the northern Kenyan rangelands. *Journal of African Economies*, 12(2), 127–155.

Barrett, C. B., Marenya, P. P., McPeak, J. *et al.* (2006). Welfare dynamics in rural Kenya and Madagascar. *The Journal of Development Studies*, 42(2), 248–277.

Barrett, C. B., Garg, T., & McBride, L. (2016). Well-being dynamics and poverty traps. *Annual Review of Resource Economics*, 8, 303–327.

Barrett, C. B., Carter, M. R., & Chavas, J. P. (Eds.). (2019). *The Economics of Poverty Traps*. Chicago: University of Chicago Press.

Bassi, M. (2005). *Decisions in the Shade: Political and Juridical Processes among the Oromo-Borana*. Trenton, NJ: The Red Sea Press.

Benami, E. & Carter, M. R. (2021). Can digital technologies reshape rural microfinance? Implications for savings, credit, & insurance. *Applied Economic Perspectives and Policy*, 43(4), 1196–1220.

Bertram-Huemmer, V. & Kraehnert, K. (2018). Does index insurance help households recover from disaster? Evidence from IBLI Mongolia. *American Journal of Agricultural Economics*, 100(1), 145–171.

Beyers, N., Chiew H., Gray, J., & Hougaard, C. (2020). *Evolving Insurance Supervisory Mandates in Sub-Saharan Africa: Implications for Data Practices*. Access to Insurance Initiative. [Online] https://a2ii.org/en/media/4879/download

Beyers, N., Gray, J., & Hougaard, C. (2018). *Regulating for Innovation*. Cenfri; FSDA. [Online] https://cenfri.org/wp-content/uploads/2018/01/Regulating-for-innovation_Cenfri-FSDA_January-2018_updated-15-March-2018.pdf

Binder, S., Klais, P., & Mußhoff, J. (2021). Global insurance pools statistics and trends: An overview of life, P&C, and health insurance. *McKinsey & Co.*

Bloom, D. E., Canning, D., & Sevilla, J. (2003). Geography and poverty traps. *Journal of Economic Growth*, 8, 355–378.

Bonds, M. H., Keenan, D. C., Rohani, P., & Sachs, J. D. (2010). Poverty trap formed by the ecology of infectious diseases. *Proceedings of the Royal Society B: Biological Sciences*, 277(1685), 1185–1192.

Boucher, S. R., Carter, M. R., Flatnes, J. E. *et al.* (2021). *Bundling Genetic and Financial Technologies for More Resilient and Productive Small-Scale Agriculture* (No. w29234). National Bureau of Economic Research.

Bowles, S., Durlauf, S. N., & Hoff, K. R. (Eds.). (2006). *Poverty traps* (pp. 116–138). New York: Russell Sage Foundation.

Browning, D. M., Snyder, K. A., & Herrick, J. E. (2019). Plant phenology: Taking the pulse of rangelands. *Rangelands*, 41(3), 129–134.

Bulte, E. & Haagsma, R. (2021). The welfare effects of index-based livestock insurance: Livestock herding on communal lands. *Environmental and Resource Economics*, 78, 587–613.

Cai, J., de Janvry, A., & Sadoulet, E. (2020). Subsidy policies and insurance demand. *The American Economic Review*, 110(8), 2422–2453.

Cai, W., Wang, G., Santoso, A. *et al.* (2015). Increased frequency of extreme La Niña events under greenhouse warming. *Nature Climate Change*, 5(2), 132–137.

Carter, M., Sugassti, M., Fava F., & Jensen, N. (2021). Measuring Quality for Sovereign Index Insurance: Concepts and a Kenyan Case Study. Working Paper, University of California, Davis.

Carter, M. R. & Barrett, C. B. (2006). The economics of poverty traps and persistent poverty: An asset-based approach. *The Journal of Development Studies*, 42(2), 178–199.

Carter, M. R. & Ikegami, M. (2009). Looking forward: Theory based measures of chronic poverty and vulnerability. In R. Addison, D. Hulme, & R. Kanbur

(Eds.), *Poverty Dynamics: Interdisciplinary Perspectives* (pp. 128–153). London: Oxford University Press.

Carter, M. R. & Chiu, T. (2018a). Quality standards for agricultural index insurance: An agenda for action. *The State of Microinsurance*, (4).

Carter, M. R. & Chiu, T. (2018b). A Minimum Quality Standard to Ensure Index Insurance Contracts Do No Harm. Feed the Future Innovation Lab for Assets and Market Access 2018-04. https://basis.ucdavis.edu/sites/g/files/dgvnsk466/files/2018-03/AMA%20brief%202018-04%20-%20Carter%20MQS%20index%20insurance-WEB.pdf.

Carter, M. R., de Janvry, A., Sadoulet, E., & Sarris, A. (2017). Index insurance for developing country agriculture: A reassessment. *Annual Review of Resource Economics*, 9, 421–438.

Carter, M. R., Jensen, N., Hobbs, A., Lepariyo, W., & Geyi, Z. (2018). A Randomized Evaluation of an Integrated Graduation and Contingent Social Protection Program in Kenya. https://basis.ucdavis.edu/project/randomized-evaluation-integrated-graduation-and-contingent-social-protection-program-kenya on July 10, 2022.

Castaing, P. & Gazeaud, J. (2022). Do Index Insurance Programs Live Up to Their Promises? Aggregating Evidence from Multiple Experiments. Working paper, The World Bank.

Catley, A. & Iyasu, A. (2010). *Moving Up or Moving Out? A Rapid Livelihoods and Conflict Analysis in Mieso-Mulu Woreda, Shinile Zone, Somali Region, Ethiopia*. Boston: Tufts University.

Catley, A., Lind, J., & Scoones, I. (2013). *Pastoralism and Development in Africa: Dynamic Change at the Margins* (p. 328). Oxfordshire: Taylor & Francis.

Ceballos, F., Kramer, B., & Robles, M. (2019). The feasibility of picture-based insurance (PBI): Smartphone pictures for affordable crop insurance. *Development Engineering*, 4, 100042.

Cerruti, H. C. (2021). Concept Project Information Document (PID) – De-risking, Inclusion and Value Enhancement of Pastoral Economies in the Horn of Africa – P176517 (English). Washington, DC: World Bank Group. http://documents.worldbank.org/curated/en/245561625088740444/Concept-Project-Information-Document-PID-De-risking-inclusion-and-value-enhancement-of-pastoral-economies-in-the-Horn-of-Africa-P176517

Chantarat, S., Barrett, C. B., Mude, A. G., & Turvey, C. G. (2007). Using weather index insurance to improve drought response for famine prevention. *American Journal of Agricultural Economics*, 89(5), 1262–1268.

Chantarat, S., Turvey, C. G., Mude, A. G., & Barrett, C. B. (2008). Improving humanitarian response to slow-onset disasters using famine-indexed weather derivatives. *Agricultural Finance Review*, 68, 169–195.

Chantarat, S., Turvey, C. G., Mude, A. G., & Barrett, C. B. (2011). Improving humanitarian response to slow-onset disasters using famine indexed weather derivatives. *Agricultural Finance Review, Forthcoming.*

Chantarat, S., Mude, A. G., Barrett, C. B., & Carter, M. R. (2013). Designing index-based livestock insurance for managing asset risk in northern Kenya. *Journal of Risk and Insurance*, 80(1), 205–237.

Chantarat, S., Mude, A. G., Barrett, C. B., & Turvey, C. G. (2017). Welfare impacts of index insurance in the presence of a poverty trap. *World Development*, 94, 119–138.

Chelanga, P., Khalai, D. C., Fava, F., & Mude, A. (2017). Determining insurable units for index-based livestock insurance in northern Kenya and southern Ethiopia. ILRI (aka ILCA and ILRAD).

Chelanga, P., Fava, F., Alulu, V. *et al.* (2022). KAZNET: An Open-Source, Micro-Tasking Platform for Remote Locations. *Frontiers in Sustainable Food Systems*, 6, 730836.

Cheng, Y., Vrieling, A., Fava, F. *et al.* (2020). Phenology of short vegetation cycles in a Kenyan rangeland from PlanetScope and Sentinel-2. *Remote Sensing of Environment*, 248, 112004.

Clarke, D. (2016). A theory of rational demand for index insurance. *American Economic Journal: Microeconomics*, 8, 283–306.

Clarke, D. J. & Lung, F. (2015). Should Governments Support the Development of Agricultural Insurance Markets? Private Sector Development Blog, https://blogs.worldbank.org/psd/should-governments-support-development-agricultural-insurance-markets

Clarke, D. J., Mahul, O., Poulter, R., & Teh, T. L. (2017). Evaluating sovereign disaster risk finance strategies: A framework. *The Geneva Papers on Risk and Insurance-Issues and Practice*, 42, 565–584.

Cole, S., Giné, X., & Vickery, J. (2017). How does risk management influence production decisions? Evidence from a field experiment. *The Review of Financial Studies*, 30(6), 1935–1970.

Coppock, D. L. (1994) The Borana plateau of southern Ethiopia: Ssynthesis of pastoral research, development, and change, 1980–91. Systems Study Number 5. Addis Ababa: ILCA.

Coppock, D. L., Fernandez-Gimenez, M., Hiernaux, P. *et al.* (2017). Rangeland Systems in Developing Nations: Conceptual Advances and Societal Implications. In Briske D. D. (Ed.), *Rangeland Systems: Processes, Management, and Challenges* (pp. 569–641). Springer Series on Environmental Management. Cham: Springer Nature.

Dasgupta, P. (1997). Nutritional status, the capacity for work, and poverty traps. *Journal of Econometrics*, 77(1), 5–37.

de Leeuw, J., Osano, P., Said, M. *et al.* (2019). The pastoral farming system: Balancing between tradition and transition. In J. Dixon, D. P. Garrity, J.-M. Boffa, T. O. Williams, *et al.* (Eds.), *Farming Systems and Food Security in Africa: Priorities for Science and Policy under Global Change* (pp. 318–353). New York: Routledge

De Oto, L., Vrieling, A., Fava, F., & de Bie, K. (2019). Exploring improvements to the design of an operational seasonal forage scarcity index from NDVI time series for livestock insurance in East Africa. *International Journal of Applied Earth Observation and Geoinformation*, 82, 101885.

Dercon, S. (Ed.). (2004). *Insurance against Poverty*. Oxford: Oxford University Press.

Doi, T., Behera, S. K., & Yamagata, T. (2022). On the predictability of the extreme drought in East Africa during the short rains season. *Geophysical Research Letters*, 49, e2022GL100905, https://doi.org/10.1029/2022GL100905

Doss, C., McPeak, J., & Barrett, C. B. (2008). Interpersonal, intertemporal and spatial variation in risk perceptions: Evidence from East Africa. *World Development*, 36(8), 1453–1468.

Dror, I., Maheshwari, S., & Mude, A. G. (2015). Using satellite data to insure camels, cows, sheep and goats: IBLI and the development of the world's first insurance for African pastoralists. Nairobi: ILRI.

Dupas, P. (2014). Short-run subsidies and long-run adoption of new health products: Evidence from a field experiment. *Econometrica*, 82(1), 197–228.

Elabed, G. & Carter, M. R. (2015). Compound-risk aversion, ambiguity and the willingness to pay for microinsurance. *Journal of Economic Behavior and Organization*, 118, 150–166.

Elabed, G., Bellemare, M. F., Carter, M. R., & Guirkinger, C. (2013). Managing basis risk with multiscale index insurance. *Agricultural Economics*, 44(4–5), 419–431.

Enenkel, M., Osgood, D., Anderson, M. *et al.* (2019). Exploiting the convergence of evidence in satellite data for advanced weather index insurance design. *Weather, Climate, and Society*, 11, 65–93

Fafchamps, M. (2003). *Rural Poverty, Risk and Development*. Cheltenham: Edward Elgar.

Fava, F. & Vrieling, A. (2021). Earth observation for drought risk financing in pastoral systems of sub-Saharan Africa. *Current Opinion in Environmental Sustainability*, 48, 44–52.

Fava, F., Upton, J., Banerjee, R., Taye, M., & Mude, A. (2018). Pre-feasibility Study for Index-Based Livestock Insurance in Niger. *ILRI Research Report 51*. Nairobi: International Livestock Research Institute (ILRI).

Fava, F., Banerjee, R., Kahiu, N. *et al.* (2020). Strengthening financial resilience to drought: A feasibility study for an index-based drought risk financing solution for pastoralists in Senegal. *Under publication.*

Fava, F., Jensen, N., Sina, J., Mude, A., & Maher, B. (2021). *Building Financial Resilience in Pastoral Communities in Africa: Lessons Learned from Implementing the Kenya Livestock Insurance* Program (KLIP). Washington, DC: World Bank Group. http://documents.worldbank.org/curated/en/88893 1613729186587/Building-Financial-Resilience-in-Pastoral-Communities-in-Africa-Lessons-Learned-from-Implementing-the-Kenya-Livestock-Insurance-Program-KLIP

Feed the Future Innovation Lab for Market, Risk & Resilience. (2021). From Climate Change to Conflict Mitigation through Insurance in East Africa. MRR Innovation Lab Project Brief. https://basis.ucdavis.edu/sites/g/files/ dgvnsk466/files/2022-04/MRR%20project%20in-brief%20-%20Harrison% 20Ethiopia%20and%20Kenya.pdf

Fischer, G., Karlan, D., McConnell, M., & Raffler, P. (2019). Short-term subsidies and seller type: A health products experiment in Uganda. *Journal of Development Economics*, 137, 110–124.

Frölich, M., Meller, M., Zoch, A., Montresor, G., & Kreutz, K. (2019). Evaluation of the Satellite Index Insurance for Pastoralists in Ethiopia (SIIPE) Programme: Impact Evaluation of the SIIPE Pilot (2017 – 2019). WFP Evaluation Report.

Funk, C., Nicholson, S. E., Landsfeld, M. *et al.* (2015). The centennial trends greater horn of Africa precipitation dataset. *Scientific Data*, 2(1), 1–17.

Galvin, K. A., Ellis, J., Boone, R. B. *et al.* (2002). Compatibility of pastoralism and conservation? A test case for using integrated assessment in the Ngorongoro conservation area, Tanzania. In D. Chatty & M. Colester (Eds.), *Displacement, Forced Settlement and Conservation* (pp. 36–60). Oxford: Berghahn Books.

Ghatak, M. (2015). Theories of poverty traps and anti-poverty policies. *The World Bank Economic Review*, 29(supplement 1), S77–S105.

Government of Kenya. (2014). Kenya: Situation Analysis for a National Agricultural Insurance Policy. Government of Kenya, Ministry of Agriculture, Livestock and Fisheries.

Greter, H., Jean-Richard, V., Crump, L. *et al.* (2014). The benefits of "One Health" for pastoralists in Africa: Proceedings. *Onderstepoort Journal of Veterinary Research*, 81(2), 1–3.

Hammonds, T. & Banerjee, R. (2018). A Business Strategy for the Distribution of Index-Based Livestock Insurance to Urban Professionals – Insights from Kenya. ILRI Research Brief 88. Nairobi: ILRI.

Hazell, P. B. (1992). The appropriate role of agricultural insurance in developing countries. *Journal of International Development*, 4(6), 567–581.

Hermans, F., Stuiver, M., Beers, P. J., & Kok, K. (2013). The distribution of roles and functions for upscaling and outscaling innovations in agricultural innovation systems. *Agricultural Systems*, 115, 117–128.

Hill, R. V., Kumar, N., Magnan, N. *et al.* (2019). Ex ante and ex post effects of hybrid index insurance in Bangladesh. *Journal of Development Economics*, 136, 1–17.

Homewood, K. (2008). *Ecology of African Pastoralist Societies*. Oxford: James Curry.

Ikegami, M., Carter, M. R., Barrett, C. B., & Janzen, S. (2019). Poverty traps and the social protection paradox. In C. B. Barrett, M. R. Carter, J. Chavas (Eds.), *The Economics of Poverty Traps* (pp. 223–256). Chicago: University of Chicago Press.

Iliffe, J. (1987). *The African Poor: A History*. Cambridge: Cambridge University Press.

Inoue, T., Nagai, S., Kobayashi, H., & Koizumi, H. (2015). Utilization of ground-based digital photography for the evaluation of seasonal changes in the aboveground green biomass and foliage phenology in a grassland ecosystem. *Ecological Informatics*, 25, 1–9.

Insurance Regulatory Authority [IRA Kenya]. (2011). Corporate Governance Guidelines for Insurance and Reinsurance Companies. www.ira.go.ke/index .php/regulatory-framework/prodential-guidelines/guidelines-to-insurers? start=20 on May 17, 2023.

Insurance Regulatory Authority [IRA Kenya]. (2015). The Kenya Index-based Insurance Policy Paper. www.ira.go.ke/images/docs/THE_DRAFT_KENYA_ INDEX_BASED_INSURANCE_POLICY_PAPER_2015.pdf

Jalan, J. & Ravallion, M. (2002). Geographic poverty traps? A micro model of consumption growth in rural China. *Journal of Applied Econometrics*, 17(4), 329–346.

Janzen, S. A. & Carter, M. R. (2019). After the drought: The impact of micro-insurance on consumption smoothing and asset protection. *American Journal of Agricultural Economics*, 101(3), 651–671.

Janzen, S. A., Carter, M. R., & Ikegami, M. (2021). Can insurance alter poverty dynamics and reduce the cost of social protection in developing countries? *Journal of Risk and Insurance*, 88(2), 293–324.

Jensen, N., Stoeffler, Q., Fava, F. *et al.* (2019). Does the design matter? Comparing satellite-based indices for insuring pastoralists against drought. *Ecological Economics*, 162, 59–73.

Jensen, N. D. & Barrett, C. (2017). Agricultural index insurance for development. *Applied Economic Perspectives and Policy*, 39(2), 199–219.

Jensen, N. D., Barrett, C. B., & Mude, A. G. (2015). The Favourable Impacts of Index-Based Livestock Insurance: Evaluation Results from Ethiopia and Kenya. ILRI Research Brief 52. Nairobi: ILRI.

Jensen, N. D., Barrett, C. B., & Mude, A. G. (2016). Index insurance quality and basis risk: Evidence from northern Kenya. *American Journal of Agricultural Economics*, 98(5), 1450–1469.

Jensen, N. D., Barrett, C. B., & Mude, A. G. (2017). Cash transfers and index insurance: A comparative impact analysis from northern Kenya. *Journal of Development Economics*, 129, 14–28.

Jensen, N. D., Ikegami, M., & Mude, A. (2017). Integrating social protection strategies for improved impact: A comparative evaluation of cash transfers and index insurance in Kenya. *The Geneva Papers on Risk and Insurance-Issues and Practice*, 42, 675–707.

Jensen, N. D., Mude, A. G., & Barrett, C. B. (2018). How basis risk and spatiotemporal adverse selection influence demand for index insurance: Evidence from northern Kenya. *Food Policy*, 74, 172–198.

Johansson, M. U., Abebe, F. B., Nemomissa, S., Bekele, T., & Hylander, K. (2021). Ecosystem restoration in fire-managed savanna woodlands: Effects on biodiversity, local livelihoods, and fire intensity. *Ambio*, 50, 190–202.

John, F., Toth, R., Frank, K., Groeneveld, J., & Müller, B. (2019). Ecological vulnerability through insurance? Potential unintended consequences of livestock drought insurance. *Ecological Economics*, 157, 357–368.

Johnson, L., Wandera, B., Jensen, N. & Banerjee, R. (2019). Competing expectations in an index-based livestock insurance project. *The Journal of Development Studies*, 55(6), 1221–1239.

Karlan, D., Osei, R., Osei-Akoto, I., & Udry, C. (2014). Agricultural decisions after relaxing credit and risk constraints. *The Quarterly Journal of Economics*, 129(2), 597–652.

Kenduiywo, B. K., Carter, M. R., Ghosh, A., & Hijmans, R. J. (2021). Evaluating the quality of remote sensing products for agricultural index insurance. *PLoS One*, 16(10), e0258215.

Kraay, A. & McKenzie, D. (2014). Do poverty traps exist? Assessing the evidence. *Journal of Economic Perspectives*, 28(3), 127–148.

Krishna, A. (2010). *One Illness Away: Why People Become Poor and How They Escape Poverty*. Oxford: Oxford University Press.

Leblois, A. & Quirion, P. (2013). Agricultural insurances based on meteorological indices: Realizations, methods and research challenges. *Meteorological Applications*, 20, 1–9.

Liebmann, B., Hoerling, M. P., Funk, C. *et al.* (2014). Understanding recent eastern Horn of Africa rainfall variability and change. *Journal of Climate*, 27(23), 8630–8645. https://doi.org/10.1175/JCLI-D-13-00714.1

Lind, J., Okenwa, D., & Scoones, I. (Eds.). (2020). *Land, Investment & Politics: Reconfiguring Eastern Africa's Pastoral Drylands* (Vol. 40). Suffolk: Boydell & Brewer.

Lind, J., Sabates-Wheeler, R., Caravani, M., Kuol, L. B., & Nightingale, D. M. (2020). Newly evolving pastoral and post-pastoral rangelands of Eastern Africa. *Pastoralism: Research, Policy and Practice*. https://doi.org/10.1186/s13570-020-00179-w

Lipton, M. & Ravallion, M. (1995). Poverty and policy. In J. Behrman & T. Srinivasan (Eds.), *Handbook of Development Economics, Volume 3*, 2551–2657. Amsterdam: Elsevier.

Little, P. D., Smith, K., Cellarius, B. A., Coppock, D. L., & Barrett, C. (2001). Avoiding disaster: Diversification and risk management among East African herders. *Development and Change*, 32(3), 401–433.

Liu, D., He, D., & Norton, T. (2020). Automatic estimation of dairy cattle body condition score from depth image using ensemble model. *Biosystems Engineering*, 194, 16–27.

Lung, F., Stutley, C., Kahiu, N. *et al.* (2021). A Regional Approach to Drought Index-Insurance in Intergovernmental Authority on Development (IGAD) Countries: Volume 1 Main Report – Operational and Technical Feasibility Assessment. *ILRI Research Report 75*. Nairobi: ILRI. https://cgspace.cgiar.org/handle/10568/114255

Luseno, W. K., McPeak, J. G., Barrett, C. B., Little, P. D., & Gebru, G. (2003). Assessing the value of climate forecast information for pastoralists: Evidence from Southern Ethiopia and Northern Kenya. *World Development*, 31(9), 1477–1494.

Lybbert, T. J., Barrett, C. B., Desta, S., & Layne Coppock, D. (2004). Stochastic wealth dynamics and risk management among a poor population. *The Economic Journal*, 114(498), 750–777.

Mahul, O. & Skees, J. (2007). Managing agricultural risk at the country level: The case of index-based livestock insurance in Mongolia. *World Bank Policy Research Working Paper*, (4325).

Mahul, O. & Stutley, C. J. (2010). *Government Support to Agricultural Insurance: Challenges and Options for Developing Countries*. World Bank.

Marsh, T. L., Yoder, J., Deboch, T., McElwain, T. F., & Palmer, G. H. (2016). Livestock vaccinations translate into increased human capital and school attendance by girls. *Science Advances*, 2(12), e1601410.

Matsaert, H., Kariuki, J., & Mude, A. (2011). Index-based livestock insurance for Kenyan pastoralists: An innovation systems perspective. *Development in Practice*, 21(3), 343–356.

Matsuda, A., Takahashi, K., & Ikegami, M. (2019). Direct and indirect impact of index-based livestock insurance in Southern Ethiopia. *The Geneva Papers on Risk and Insurance-Issues and Practice*, 44, 481–502.

Maundu, P., Kibet, S., Morimoto, Y., Imbumi, M., & Adeka, R. (2009). Impact of Prosopis juliflora on Kenya's semi-arid and arid ecosystems and local livelihoods. *Biodiversity*, 10(2–3), 33–50.

Mburu, S., Johnson, L., & Mude, A. (2015). Integrating index-based livestock insurance with community savings and loan groups in northern Kenya. ILRI Research Brief 60. Nairobi: ILRI.

McCarthy, N., Swallow, B., Kirk, M., & Hazell, P. (2000). Property Rights, Risk, and Livestock Development in Africa. *Nairobi, Kenya: International Livestock Research Institute, Washington, DC: International Food Policy Research Institute.*

McLeod, A. & Kristjanson, R. (1999). Impact of Ticks and Associated Diseases on Cattle in Asia, Australia, and Africa. ILRI and eSYS Report to ACIAR. *International Livestock Research Institute, Nairobi, Kenya.*

McPeak, J. G. & Barrett, C. B. (2001). Differential risk exposure and stochastic poverty traps among East African pastoralists. *American Journal of Agricultural Economics*, 83(3), 674–679.

McPeak, J. G., Chantarat, S., & Mude, A. (2010). Explaining index-based livestock insurance to pastoralists. *Agricultural Finance Review*, 70(3), 333–352.

McPeak, J. G., Little, P. D., & Doss, C. R. (2011). *Risk and Social Change in an African Rural Economy: Livelihoods in Pastoralist Communities.* New York: Routledge.

Meroni, M., Fasbender, D., Kayitakire, F. *et al.* (2014). Early detection of biomass production deficit hot-spots in semi-arid environment using FAPAR time series and a probabilistic approach. *Remote Sensing of Environment*, 142, 57–68.

Meroni, M., Ng, W. T., Rembold, F. *et al.* (2017). Mapping Prosopis juliflora in west Somaliland with Landsat 8 satellite imagery and ground information. *Land Degradation & Development*, 28(2), 494–506.

Mills, C. J., Jensen, N. D., Barrett, C. B., & Mude, A. G. (2016). Characterization for index-based livestock insurance. *ILRI Research Report 39.* Nairobi: ILRI.

Mookherjee, D. & Ray, D. (2002). Contractual structure and wealth accumulation. *American Economic Review*, 92(4), 818–849.

Mude, A. (2017). The Role of Mobile Technologies in Promoting Sustainable Delivery of Livestock Insurance in the East African Drylands: Toward Sustainable Index-Based Livestock Insurance (IBLI) for Pastoralists. Presented at the Crawford Fund Annual Conference, Canberra, August 7–8, 2017. Nairobi: ILRI. https://hdl.handle.net/10568/83080

Mude, A. G., Barrett, C. B., McPeak, J. G., Kaitho, R., & Kristjanson, P. (2009). Empirical forecasting of slow-onset disasters for improved emergency response: An application to Kenya's arid north. *Food Policy*, 34(4), 329–339.

Müller, B., Johnson, L., & Kreuer, D. (2017). Maladaptive outcomes of climate insurance in agriculture. *Global Environmental Change*, 46, 23–33.

Munyao, K. & Barrett C. B. (2007). Decentralization of pastoral resources management and its effects on environmental degradation and poverty: Experience from northern Kenya. In C. B. Barrett, A. G. Mude, & J. M. Omiti (Eds.), *Decentralization and the Social Economics of Development: Lessons from Kenya* (1st ed., pp. 97–110). Wallingford: CABI. https://doi.org/10.1079/9781845932695.0097

Mutai, C. C. & Ward, M. N. (2000). East African rainfall and the tropical circulation/convection on intraseasonal to interannual timescales. *Journal of Climate*, 13(22), 3915–3939.

Ngonghala, C. N., Pluciński, M. M., Murray, M. B. *et al.* (2014). Poverty, disease, and the ecology of complex systems. *PLoS Biology*, 12(4), e1001827.

Ngonghala, C. N., De Leo, G. A., Pascual, M. M. *et al.* (2017). General ecological models for human subsistence, health, and poverty. *Nature Ecology & Evolution*, 1(8), 1153–1159.

Nidumolu, U., Gobbett, D., Hayman, P. *et al.* (2022). Climate change shifts agropastoral-pastoral margins in Africa putting food security and livelihoods at risk. *Environmental Research Letters*, 17(9), 095003.

Nikulkov, A., Barrett, C. B., Mude, A. G., & Wein, L. M. (2016). Assessing the impact of US food assistance delivery policies on child mortality in northern Kenya. *PloS One*, 11(12), e0168432.

Nobre, G. G., Davenport, F., Bischiniotis, K. *et al.* (2019). Financing agricultural drought risk through ex ante cash transfers. *Science of the Total Environment*, 653, 523–535.

Noritomo, Y. & Takahashi, K. (2020). Can insurance payouts prevent a poverty trap? Evidence from randomised experiments in Northern Kenya. *The Journal of Development Studies*, 56(11), 2079–2096.

Organization for Economic Co-operation and Development (OECD). (2023). Enhancing the Insurance Sector's Contribution to Climate Adaptation, OECD Business and Finance Policy Papers, No. 26, Paris: OECD, https://doi.org/10.1787/0951dfcd-en

Osgood, D. & Enenkel, M. (2020, May). The Next Generation Drought Index Project, EGU General Assembly 2020, Online, May 4–8, 2020, EGU2020-12023, https://doi.org/10.5194/egusphere-egu2020-12023

Osgood, D., Powell, B., Diro, R. *et al.* (2018). Farmer perception, recollection, and remote sensing in weather index insurance: An Ethiopia case study. *Remote Sensing*, 10(12), 1887.

Ouma, R., Mude, A., & van de Steeg, J. (2011). Dealing with climate-related risks: Some pioneering ideas for enhanced pastoral risk management in Africa. *Experimental Agriculture*, 47(2), 375–393.

Overpeck, J. T. & Udall, B. (2020). Climate change and the aridification of North America. *Proceedings of the National Academy of Sciences*, 117(22), 11856–11858.

Patt, A., Peterson, N., Carter, M. *et al.* (2009). Making index insurance attractive to farmers. *Mitigation and Adaptation Strategies for Global Change*, 14, 737–753.

Pinzón, J. E., & Tucker, C. J. (2014). A non-stationary 1981–2012 AVHRR NDVI3g time series. *Remote Sensing*, 6(8), 6929–6960.

Ravallion, M. (2016). *The Economics of Poverty: History, Measurement, and Policy.* Oxford: Oxford University Press.

Reid, R. S., Nkedianye, D., Said, M. Y. *et al.* (2016). Evolution of models to support community and policy action with science: Balancing pastoral livelihoods and wildlife conservation in savannas of East Africa. *Proceedings of the National Academy of Sciences*, 113(17), 4579–4584.

Roumiguié, A., Sigel, G., Poilvé, H. *et al.* (2017). Insuring forage through satellites: Testing alternative indices against grassland production estimates for France. *International Journal of Remote Sensing*, 38(7), 1912–1939.

Sakketa, T. G. & Kornher, L. (2021). *Unintended Consequences or a Glimmer of Hope? Comparative Impact Analysis of Cash Transfers and Index Insurance on Pastoralists' Labor Allocation Decisions* [Conference presentation]. International Conference of Agricultural Economics, Online. https://doi.org/10.22004/ag.econ.315113

Santos, P. & Barrett, C. B. (2011). Persistent poverty and informal credit. *Journal of Development Economics*, 96(2), 337–347.

Santos, P. & Barrett, C. B. (2019). Heterogeneous wealth dynamics: On the roles of risk and ability. In C. B. Barrett, M. R. Carter, & J.-P. Chavas (Eds.), *The Economics of Poverty Traps* (pp. 265–290). Chicago: University of Chicago Press.

Scholer, M. & Schuermans, P. (2022). Climate change adaptation in insurance. In C. Kondrup, P. Mercogliano, F. Bosello *et al.* (Eds.), *Climate Adaptation Modelling: Springer Climate* (pp. 187–194). Cham: Springer. https://doi.org/10.1007/978-3-030-86211-4_22

Schut, M., Leeuwis, C., & Thiele, G. (2020). Science of scaling: Understanding and guiding the scaling of innovation for societal outcomes. *Agricultural Systems*, 184, 102908.

Signé, L. & Johnson, C. (2020). Africa's insurance potential: Trends, drivers, opportunities and strategies. Research Paper, November 2020, Policy Center for the New South.

Skakun, S., Justice, C. O., Vermote, E., & Roger, J. C. (2018). Transitioning from MODIS to VIIRS: An analysis of inter-consistency of NDVI data sets for agricultural monitoring. *International Journal of Remote Sensing*, 39(4), 971–992.

Smith, A. (1776). *The Wealth of Nations: An Inquiry into the Nature and Causes of the Wealth of Nations*. London: W. Strahan and T. Cadell.

Smith, K., Barrett, C. B., & Box, P. W. (2000). Participatory risk mapping for targeting research and assistance: With an example from East African pastoralists. *World Development*, 28(11), 1945–1959.

Son, H. H. (2022). The effect of microinsurance on child work and schooling. *Unpublished manuscript.*

St. Claire, M. & Banerjee, R. 2019. Monitoring, evaluating, and learning for education and extension–a framework for Index Based Livestock Insurance. Extension Brief. International Livestock Research Institute.

Stiglitz, J. (1974). Incentives and risk sharing in sharecropping. *Review of Economic Studies*, 41(2), 219–255.

Swinnen, E. & Veroustraete, F. (2008). Extending the SPOT-VEGETATION NDVI time series (1998–2006) back in time with NOAA-AVHRR data (1985–1998) for Southern Africa. *IEEE Transactions on Geoscience and Remote Sensing*, 46(2), 558–572.

Tafere, K., Barrett, C. B., & Lentz, E. (2019). Insuring well-being? Buyer's remorse and peace of mind effects from insurance. *American Journal of Agricultural Economics*, 101(3), 627–650.

Takahashi, K., Ikegami, M., Sheahan, M., & Barrett, C. B. (2016). Experimental evidence on the drivers of index-based livestock insurance demand in Southern Ethiopia. *World Development*, 78, 324–340.

Takahashi, K., Barrett, C. B., & Ikegami, M. (2019). Does index insurance crowd in or crowd out informal risk sharing? Evidence from rural Ethiopia. *American Journal of Agricultural Economics*, 101(3), 672–691.

Takahashi, K., Noritomo, Y., Ikegami, M., & Jensen, N. D. (2020). Understanding pastoralists' dynamic insurance uptake decisions: Evidence from four-year panel data in Ethiopia. *Food Policy*, 95, 101910.

Taye, M. (2022). *Financialisation of Risk among the Borana Pastoralists of Ethiopia: Practices of Integrating Livestock Insurance in Responding to Risk*, PhD dissertation, Institute of Development Studies, University of Sussex, Brighton.

Taye, M. (2023). Livestock insurance in Southern Ethiopia: Calculating risks, responding to uncertainties. In J. Scoones (Ed.), *Pastoralism, Uncertainty and Development* (pp. 93–106). Rugby: Practical Action.

Taye, M. & Jensen, N. (2019). Using mLearning to improve training retention: Lessons from Ethiopia. Research Brief 92. Nairobi: ILRI.

Taye, M., Alulu, V., Gobu, W., & Jensen, N. D. (2019). Livestock insurance payouts and coping strategies of pastoralists during drought. ILRI Research Brief 90. Nairobi: ILRI.

Thebaud, B. (2016). The Feasibility of Index-Based Livestock Insurance (IBLI) in the West African Sahel: Framing the Issue. Report by Life-Nordic Consulting Group, accessed on June 10, 2022 from www.celep.info/wp-content/uploads/2017/11/2016-Thebaud-AFL-Feasibilty-IBLI-in-WA.pdf

Toth, R. (2015). Traps and thresholds in pastoralist mobility. *American Journal of Agricultural Economics*, 97(1), 315–332.

Toth, R., Barrett, C. B., Bernstein, R. *et al.* (2017). Behavioural substitution of formal risk mitigation: Index insurance in East Africa. *Unpublished manuscript*.

Udelhoven, T., Stellmes, M., Del Barrio, G., & Hill, J. (2009). Assessment of rainfall and NDVI anomalies in Spain (1989–1999) using distributed lag models. *International Journal of Remote Sensing*, 30, 1961–1976.

Vrieling, A., Meroni, M., Shee, A. *et al.* (2014). Historical extension of operational NDVI products for livestock insurance in Kenya. *International Journal of Applied Earth Observation and Geoinformation*, 28, 238–251.

Vrieling, A., Meroni, M., Mude, A. G. *et al.* (2016). Early assessment of seasonal forage availability for mitigating the impact of drought on East African pastoralists. *Remote Sensing of Environment*, 174, 44–55.

Vrieling, A., Fava, F., Leitner, S. *et al.* (2022). Identification of temporary livestock enclosures in Kenya from multi-temporal PlanetScope imagery. *Remote Sensing of Environment*, 279, 113110.

Vroege, W., Vrieling, A., & Finger, R. (2021). Satellite support to insure farmers against extreme droughts. *Nature Food*, 2(4), 215–217.

Wandera, B., Kang'ethe, E., & Davies, B. (2015). Mobile technology-driven capacity development: Lessons from the mNutrition and IBLI projects. ILRI Capacity Development Brief 3. Nairobi: ILRI.

Wang, D., Morton, D., Masek, J. *et al.* (2012). Impact of sensor degradation on the MODIS NDVI time series. *Remote Sensing of Environment*, 119, 55–61.

Watts, M. (1983). *Silent Violence: Food, Famine, and Peasantry in Northern Nigeria*. Oakland: University of California Press.

Weingärtner, L., & Wilkinson, E. (2019). *Anticipatory Crisis Financing and Action: Concepts, Initiatives and Evidence*. London: Centre for Disaster Protection.

West, H., Quinn, N., & Horswell, M. (2019). Remote sensing for drought monitoring & impact assessment: Progress, past challenges, and future opportunities. *Remote Sensing of Environment*, 232, 111291.

Western, D., Russell, S., & Cuthill, I. (2009). The status of wildlife in protected areas compared to non-protected areas of Kenya. *PloS One*, 4(7), e6140.

Western, D., Tyrrell, P., Brehony, P. *et al.* (2020). Conservation from the inside-out: Winning space and a place for wildlife in working landscapes. *People and Nature*, 2(2), 279–291.

Wilcox, S., Barrett, C., Clark, P. *et al.* (2023). Index based livestock insurance and rangeland health: Evidence from Kenya and Ethiopia. *Unpublished manuscript*.

Wild, H., Glowacki, L., Maples, S. *et al.* (2019). Making pastoralists count: Geospatial methods for the health surveillance of nomadic populations. *The American Journal of Tropical Medicine and Hygiene*, 101(3), 661.

Williams, A. P. & Funk, C. (2011). A westward extension of the warm pool leads to a westward extension of the Walker circulation, drying eastern Africa. *Climate Dynamics*, 37, 2417–2435.

World Bank Group (WBG). (2015). Kenya toward a National Crop and Livestock Insurance Program: Background Report. Washington, DC: World Bank. https://openknowledge.worldbank.org/handle/10986/24444

World Bank Group (WBG). (2022). De-risking, Inclusion and Value Enhancement of Pastoral Economies in the Horn of Africa Project. Project Appraisal Document. Washington, DC: World Bank. https://documents1 .worldbank.org/curated/en/465961658500251418/pdf/Djibouti-Kenya-Ethiopia-and-Somalia-De-risking-Inclusion-and-Value-Enhancement-of-Pastoral-Economies-in-the-Horn-of-Africa-Project.pdf

World Food Programme (WFP). (2021). WFP Ethiopia Country Brief: July 2021. WFP.

World Food Programme (WFP). (2022). 2021 Climate Risk Insurance Annual Report. Rome: WFP. www.wfp.org/publications/2021-climate-risk-insurance-annual-report

Xiao, Z., Liang, S., Tian, X. *et al.* (2017). Reconstruction of long-term temporally continuous NDVI and surface reflectance from AVHRR data. *IEEE Journal of Selected Topics in Applied Earth Observations and Remote Sensing*, 10(12), 5551–5556.

Zhao, S. & Cook, K. H. (2021). Influence of Walker circulations on East African rainfall. *Climate Dynamics*, 56, 2127–2147. https://doi.org/10.1007/s00382-020-05579-7

Author Contributions Statement

The authors confirm their contribution to the manuscript as follows. NJ, FF, AM, and CB led the manuscript's conceptualization and coordination. NJ, FF, AM, CB, AV, FL, RB contributed considerably to the manuscript in its entirety. NJ, FF, AM, CB, BW, AV, MT, KT, FL, MI, PE, PC, SC, MC, HB, and RB developed the contents for specific sections. Authorship order reflects the leadership provided by NJ, FF, AM, and CB followed by reverse alphabetical order.

Acknowledgments

We thank those individuals and organizations that have worked to improve, question, or support IBLI over the years, and recognize ILRI for its central role in championing the IBLI agenda. The IBLI research program received financial support from the CGIAR Research Program on Dryland Systems, the CGIAR Research Program on Climate Change, Agriculture and Food Security, the CGIAR Standing Panel on Impact Assessment, the United Kingdom Department for International Development, the United States Agency for International Development, the Australian Department of Foreign Affairs and Trade, the Japan Society for the Promotion of Science, the World Bank Group, Cornell University, Syracuse University, the University of California at Davis, the University of Sydney, and the Dutch Research Council. We also thank Amanda Lawrence-Brown for providing copy-editing support for this document and two anonymous reviewers for helpful comments. All views and interpretations expressed in this publication are those of the authors and not necessarily those of the supporting or cooperating institutions.

Cambridge Elements ≡

Development Economics

Series Editor-in-Chief

Kunal Sen
UNU-WIDER and University of Manchester

Kunal Sen, UNU-WIDER Director, is Editor-in-Chief of the Cambridge Elements in Development Economics series. Professor Sen has over three decades of experience in academic and applied development economics research, and has carried out extensive work on international finance, the political economy of inclusive growth, the dynamics of poverty, social exclusion, female labor force participation, and the informal sector in developing economies. His research has focused on India, East Asia, and sub-Saharan Africa.

In addition to his work as Professor of Development Economics at the University of Manchester, Kunal has been the Joint Research Director of the Effective States and Inclusive Development Research Centre, and a Research Fellow at the Institute for Labor Economics (IZA). He has also served in advisory roles with national governments and bilateral and multilateral development agencies, including the UK's Department for International Development, Asian Development Bank, and the International Development Research Centre.

Thematic Editors

Tony Addison
University of Copenhagen and UNU-WIDER

Tony Addison is a Professor of Economics in the University of Copenhagen's Development Economics Research Group. He is also a Non-Resident Senior Research Fellow at UNU-WIDER, Helsinki, where he was previously the Chief Economist-Deputy Director. In addition, he is Professor of Development Studies at the University of Manchester. His research interests focus on the extractive industries, energy transition, and macroeconomic policy for development.

Chris Barrett
SC Johnson College of Business, Cornell University

Chris Barrett is an agricultural and development economist at Cornell University. He is the Stephen B. and Janice G. Ashley Professor of Applied Economics and Management; and International Professor of Agriculture at the Charles H. Dyson School of Applied Economics and Management. He is also an elected Fellow of the American Association for the Advancement of Science, the Agricultural and Applied Economics Association, and the African Association of Agricultural Economists.

Carlos Gradín
University of Vigo

Carlos Gradín is a professor of applied economics at the University of Vigo. His main research interest is the study of inequalities, with special attention to those that exist between population groups (e.g., by race or sex). His publications have contributed to improving the empirical evidence in developing and developed countries, as well as globally, and to improving the available data and methods used.

Rachel M. Gisselquist

UNU-WIDER

Rachel M. Gisselquist is a Senior Research Fellow and member of the Senior Management Team of UNU-WIDER. She specializes in the comparative politics of developing countries, with particular attention to issues of inequality, ethnic and identity politics, foreign aid and state building, democracy and governance, and sub-Saharan African politics. Dr Gisselquist has edited a dozen collections in these areas, and her articles are published in a range of leading journals.

Shareen Joshi

Georgetown University

Shareen Joshi is an Associate Professor of International Development at Georgetown University's School of Foreign Service in the United States. Her research focuses on issues of inequality, human capital investment and grassroots collective action in South Asia. Her work has been published in the fields of development economics, population studies, environmental studies and gender studies.

Patricia Justino

UNU-WIDER and IDS – UK

Patricia Justino is a Senior Research Fellow at UNU-WIDER and Professorial Fellow at the Institute of Development Studies (IDS) (on leave). Her research focuses on the relationship between political violence, governance and development outcomes. She has published widely in the fields of development economics and political economy and is the co-founder and co-director of the Households in Conflict Network.

Marinella Leone

University of Pavia

Marinella Leone is an assistant professor at the Department of Economics and Management,University of Pavia, Italy. She is an applied development economist. Her more recentre search focuses on the study of early child development parenting programmes, on education,and gender-based violence. In previous research she investigated the short-, long-term and intergenerational impact of conflicts on health, education and domestic violence. She has published in top journals in economics and development economics.

Jukka Pirttilä

University of Helsinki and UNU-WIDER

Jukka Pirttilä is Professor of Public Economics at the University of Helsinki and VATT Institute for Economic Research. He is also a Non-Resident Senior Research Fellow at UNU-WIDER. His research focuses on tax policy, especially for developing countries. He is a co-principal investigator at the Finnish Centre of Excellence in Tax Systems Research.

Andy Sumner

King's College London and UNU-WIDER

Andy Sumner is Professor of International Development at King's College London; a Non-Resident Senior Fellow at UNU-WIDER and a Fellow of the Academy of Social Sciences. He has published extensively in the areas of poverty, inequality, and economic development.

About the Series

Cambridge Elements in Development Economics is led by UNU-WIDER in partnership with Cambridge University Press. The series publishes authoritative studies on important topics in the field covering both micro and macro aspects of development economics.

United Nations University World Institute for Development Economics Research

United Nations University World Institute for Development Economics Research (UNU-WIDER) provides economic analysis and policy advice aiming to promote sustainable and equitable development for all. The institute began operations in 1985 in Helsinki, Finland, as the first research centre of the United Nations University. Today, it is one of the world's leading development economics think tanks, working closely with a vast network of academic researchers and policy makers, mostly based in the Global South.

Cambridge Elements $^{\equiv}$

Development Economics

Printed in the United States
by Baker & Taylor Publisher Services